REBUILDING THE FIRE AND RESCUE SERVICES

The authors have produced a tour de force that combines comprehensive knowledge of performance management, a holistic systemic perspective, and real affinity for the fire and rescue services and the improvement of services to the public.

Andrew Lynch, Editor of FIRE Magazine

This is an instant, knowledgeable and very practical response to some of the most urgent contemporary issues facing the leadership and management of fire and rescue services. It effortlessly transcends policy and practice with clear practical and realistic recommendations for improving this vital public service.

Paresh Wankhade, Editor: International Journal of Emergency Services, Edge Hill University, UK

In the best tradition of *Emerald Points*, this book has clear implications and lessons for policy development, the delivery of fire and rescue services and the assurance that the sector owes to the public. It should be compulsory reading for senior civil servants, chief fire officers and our regulatory colleagues.

Craig Parkin, Deputy Chief Fire Officer, Nottinghamshire Fire Service, UK

This book provides a comprehensive understanding of performance management and adopts a critical friend perspective that epitomizes the best of such a position: a rigorous critical analysis of the sector with constructive advice on how to improve.

Kirsten Greenhalgh, University of Nottingham, UK

REBUILDING THE FIRE AND RESCUE SERVICES

Policy, Delivery and Assurance

PETER MURPHY
Nottingham Trent University, UK

KATARZYNA LAKOMA
Nottingham Trent University, UK

PETER ECKERSLEY
Nottingham Trent University, UK

RUSS GLENNON
Manchester Metropolitan University, UK

United Kingdom – North America – Japan – India
Malaysia – China

Emerald Publishing Limited
Howard House, Wagon Lane, Bingley BD16 1WA, UK

First edition 2020

British Library Cataloguing in Publication Data
A catalogue record for this book is available from the British Library

ISBN: 978-1-83867-758-9 (Print)
ISBN: 978-1-83867-755-8 (Online)
ISBN: 978-1-83867-757-2 (Epub)

ISOQAR certified
Management System,
awarded to Emerald
for adherence to
Environmental
standard
ISO 14001:2004.

Certificate Number 1985
ISO 14001

INVESTOR IN PEOPLE

CONTENTS

LIST OF FIGURES

LIST OF TABLES

BIOGRAPHIES

Peter Murphy is Professor of Public Policy and Management and Head of Research at Nottingham Business School, Nottingham Trent University. He is a member of the Advisory Board of the Centre for Public Scrutiny. Prior to joining the business school, he was a senior civil servant in four Whitehall departments, a director of the Government Office for the East Midlands and Chief Executive of Melton Borough Council in Leicestershire. He was responsible for emergency planning and coordinating the response to emergencies at local, regional and national levels for over 30 years.

Katarzyna Lakoma is a Research Associate and PhD researcher in the Emergency Services Unit of the Public Policy and Research Group at Nottingham Business School, Nottingham Trent University. A graduate of Poznan University of Economics and Business and Nottingham Trent University, her PhD research relates to the governance and management of Fire and Rescue Services in the UK. She is the Assistant Editor of the *International Journal of Emergency Services*.

Peter Eckersley is Senior Research Fellow in Public Policy and Management at Nottingham Business School, Nottingham Trent University and Research Associate at the Leibniz Institute for Research on Society and Space, Erkner, Germany. He has worked at Newcastle University, the University of York and the University of Sheffield, and spent 10 years at the Chartered Institute of Public Finance and Accountancy before entering academia. His research interests are in public policy, multi-level governance and sustainability. He is an Editor of *Local Government Studies*.

Russ Glennon is Reader in Public Management and Strategy at Manchester Metropolitan University. He is a council member of the British Academy of Management and chair of its Public Management & Governance special interest group. He is also Vice Chair (Research) of the Public Administration Committee of the Joint Universities Council. Prior to joining academia, he was a senior manager in both local government and the private sector. His research interests include performance management, accountability and delivery of public services.

ACKNOWLEDGEMENTS

We would like to acknowledge and thank our families and our academic colleagues for their continuous support, patience and understanding during the writing of this book and much more.

Pete would like to thank his wife Steph, his son Rob and his doctoral supervision team of Professor David Smith, Professor Joyce Liddle and Dr Martin Jones. Chapter 2 originates from his PhD thesis.

Katarzyna would like to thank her partner Jack and especially her parents who continually supported her along her academic career.

Peter would like to thank Susannah, Abigail and Lukas for tolerating his research-related monologues with remarkable patience and understanding over the years.

Russ would like to thank his wife Jo and son Elliot.

We would all like to thank the team at Emerald and in particular, Hazel Goodes our Publisher and Anna Scaife and Krystal Ramsey our Editorial Assistants for having the confidence to commission the book and their help, support and patience in bringing it to publication.

1

ALARM BELLS RINGING:
INTRODUCTION

*It is currently almost impossible to scrutinise your
local fire and rescue service. There's no independent
inspectorate; no regular audit of performance; and
only limited available data on performance over time
or between areas.*

(May, 2016, p. 8)

Theresa May, in one of her final speeches as Home Secretary before becoming prime minister, outlined a number of major inadequacies in the performance measurement, management and monitoring of the Fire and Rescue Services in England. At the time, she was the longest serving Home Secretary since James Chuter Ede (1945–1951). Her speech was delivered at the think tank 'Reform', as had many of her speeches and those of her ministers when dealing with controversial subjects. The speech outlined her response to two highly critical reports from the National Audit Office (NAO, 2015) and the Public Accounts Select Committee (PAC, 2016), which had looked into the national oversight and management of the service by the government and more specifically the (former) Department of Communities and

Local Government under the leadership of Secretary of State Eric Pickles.

> *The Secretary of State has a statutory duty to assure Parliament on the standards of fire and rescue authorities, but DCLG's evidence to support these statements is limited. DCLG is almost entirely reliant on authorities to self-certify they are in compliance with their mandated duties.*

(NAO, 2015, p. 10)

In January 2016, in response to the NAO report, the government announced that it was transferring the responsibility for Fire and Rescue Services to the Home Office. This could be interpreted as an attempt to avoid the scrutiny by the House of Commons' Public Accounts Committee's (PAC) in the light of the NAO report. Nevertheless, as we know, the PAC insisted on investigating the state of the service and its own highly critical report was published in February 2016 (PAC, 2016).

> *The Department of Communities and Local Government's understanding of the pressures now faced by Fire and Rescue Services is seriously flawed. Without this understanding, further efficiency savings could put services at risk, potentially putting lives at risk.*
> (Meg Hillier MP. Chair of the Committee of Public Accounts statement 5 November 2015)

The committee recommended that the Home Office should write to the committee by the summer of 2016 and set out how it would be improving the central government's understanding of the impacts of ongoing funding reductions on fire and rescue authorities. This should take into account, in particular, both the fire authorities' capacity to make further efficiency savings and the impact of prevention and protection activities on fire risk (PAC, 2016, Recommendation 1. p5).

The government accepted the committee's recommendation in April 2016 (as it had in responding to the draft report earlier) and Mrs May's speech set out in some detail its strategic vision which was consciously based on a similar series of reforms to the police carried out under her stewardship of the Home Office between 2010 and 2015 (Murphy, Ferry, Glennon, & Greenhalgh, 2019; Wankhade & Weir, 2015).

Mrs May proposed to develop and incorporate appropriate amendments in the Policing and Crime Bill that was going through its final stages in Parliament at the time. Although Chapters 1–4 of the subsequent Policing and Crime Act 2017 essentially deal with changes to Fire and Rescue Services, it was too late to change the 'face' of the Bill, and Fire and Rescue is not included in the title of the Act. The Grenfell Tower Disaster occurred on 14 June 2016, the UK European Union membership referendum took place on 23 June and Mrs May became Prime Minister on 13 July 2016. The referendum, general election and appointment of Mrs May as Prime Minister not only facilitated the relatively smooth passage of the Policing and Crime Bill into the 2017 Act but also dramatically refocused the political, bureaucratic and managerial time and energy of the government and key stakeholders onto the agenda that swiftly became known as Brexit.

This book looks at the three specific aspects of the subsequent reforms that are mentioned in the opening quote from the Home Secretary over three years ago.

Chapter 2 sets out a model that demonstrates the interrelationship between the three subjects: policy development, service delivery and public assurance. It locates them in relation to the strategic and operational landscape of Fire and Rescue Services in England, the legislative parameters to action and the public resources made available to the sector. It also provides the basis for assessing the adequacy of the overall performance regime and its constituent parts.

Chapter 3 examines the state of performance data, information and intelligence available to the government, to Fire and Rescue Services, to their regulators, to stakeholders and to collaborators. The regular audit of performance and the inadequate performance data over time and between areas together with other changes required by the act demonstrated that the 2012 National Framework (DCLG, 2012) was both inadequate and obsolete. Chapter 3 looks at the evidence base available for policy development, service delivery and public assurance that was acknowledged by the government as unfit for purpose by 2016.

Chapter 4 examines the 2018 National Framework (Home Office, 2018), which replaced the 2012 framework as the performance regime for National Fire and Rescue Services. Under section 21 of the Fire and Rescue Services 2004, the Secretary of State must prepare a national framework and keep it up to date and once the NAO and PAC reports had exposed the gross inadequacy of the arrangements under the 2012 Framework, it was inevitable that it would have to be replaced (Glennon & Murphy, 2018). Although the Public Inquiry into the Grenfell Tower disaster (Moore-Bick, 2017) and Dame Judith Hackitt's enquiry into the inadequacy of building regulations (Hackitt, 2018) were both ongoing at the time, the Minister of State for Policing and the Fire Service in launching the 2018 Framework said:

> *The national framework provides the basis for how fire and rescue services in England should operate. The revised version we have published today should support them becoming more accountable, effective and professional than ever before and embed the government's reform programme.*
>
> (Nick Hurd MP. Minister for Policing and the Fire Service 8 May 2018)

Nevertheless, he acknowledged that further changes would be necessary to incorporate lessons learnt from Grenfell and from the Hackitt Report. The necessity for further improvement was highlighted on the day of publication of the Hackitt Report when the FM Global Resilience Index 2018 revealed that the UK was ranked 34th when it comes to fire resilience, below Turkey (17), Russia (21) and Bosnia (26), as well as the developed nations in the EU (FIRE, 2018). The index is intended to help risk managers understand and measure their companies' capacity to endure and respond to disruption, so they can ensure the business remains resilient. The UK's arrangements for fire resilience were considerably below the UK's other factors measured by the index such as natural hazard exposure, supply chain visibility, corruption and corporate governance quality.

The Framework did, however, include guidance on how fire and rescue authorities should work with, *inter alia*, Her Majesty's Inspectorate of Constabulary and Fire & Rescue Services (HMICFRS). The 'robust and independent' inspectorate for Fire and Rescue Service that Mrs May promised in her 2016 speech was established in July 2017 although it emerged as a remodelled Her Majesty's Inspectorate of Constabulary. HMICFRS and its first programme of fire and rescue service inspections is the subject of Chapter 5 of this book. The final chapter will then draw together some conclusions and suggest some ideas or areas for both future research and potential implications for future practice.

Before embarking on this evaluation it will be helpful to establish some basic fundamental contentions about Fire and Rescue Services in England that are held by the authors. For scholars and practitioners outside of the UK these may appear self-evident but in the UK they have recently been contested under the UK's Coalition and Conservative Governments between 2010 and 2019. By being explicit about these judgements we hope to facilitate the readers' understanding of our position and the views and recommendations that flow from our evaluations into our conclusions and suggestions for future research and practice.

The primary purpose of fire and rescue services and the **strategic intent of government** is to maintain the **safety of the public**, through the avoidance, minimisation or mitigation of fire and related incidents and the associated risks to the public. This is not contested but it is concurrent with a statutory requirement to provide public services that are as economic, efficient and effective as they can be in the circumstances, they are in. There are clearly potential conflicts between these two aspirations and in practice trade-offs have had to be made.

The work of fire and recue services also involves multiple strategic and operational collaborations with other emergency services, most notably the police and ambulance service. These include, but are not limited to, Local and National Resilience Forums, Community Safety Partnerships, Health and Wellbeing Boards and Local Safeguarding Partnerships for both Children and Adults. The common characteristic of all these collaborations is that their core purpose is the safety of the public.

The provision, evaluation and configuration of fire and rescue services should be undertaken on the basis of an assessment of the **contemporary risks to public safety** (whether to individuals to communities or to land, buildings and premises) in the short, medium and long term. This was established by the 2004 Fire and Rescue Services Act and has been operationalised through the Integrated Risk Management Planning process.

The delivery of most public services is configured on the basis of an assessment of individual or collective need, and examples include welfare, social services, education, social housing etc. Some services are provided on the basis of demand, such as leisure services, building control and transport. Some services are known as universal services because they are available and are assumed to benefit every citizen. These are often regulatory services such as trading standards, environmental health, development control or public health provision.

Fire and rescue services throughout the world are overwhelmingly and traditionally provided and configured on the basis of an assessment of risks. In the recent era of austerity in the UK, some politicians, most notably Brandon Lewis MP (previous Minister of State for Policing and the Fire Service, 2016) and his successor Nick Hurd MP (the Minister in 2019) have tried to emphasise or present the falling number of fire incidents in England as a reduction in *demand* for the service, and therefore part of a justification for continuously reducing the resources available to the service (Hurd, 2018).

Since 2010, the legislative and policy framework for Fire and Rescue Services in England has also strongly emphasised the control of costs (DCLG, 2010; Home Office, 2018) and the consequences of this change are evident in the first HMICFRS inspection reports (Murphy, 2019). Competition, commercialisation and marketisation were also prominently encouraged in the early years of the Coalition Government, via the Open Government White Paper (Cabinet Office, 2011) and the 2012 National Framework (DCLG, 2012) which for the first time was addressed solely to Fire Authorities (and not Fire Services). The 2012 National Framework differentiated the roles of the Fire Authority and Fire and Rescue Services along a commissioner/provider split with the Fire Authority being solely responsible for commissioning services while the Fire and Rescue Services (and other private companies for outsourced services) would become service providers.

Following the NAO and Public Accounts Select Committee reports, the Policing and Crime Act 2017 and the 2018 National Framework signal a shift in emphasis in how the sector's 'strategic intent' is to be delivered with **a much greater emphasis (and a formal statutory duty) on collaborations between public services** most notably (but not exclusively) collaboration between the three 'Blue Light' emergency services of fire, police and ambulance services.

This re-emphasis reinforces our fourth contention. The most promising and appropriate theoretical basis for investigating and evaluating fire and rescue services is the adoption of a **public value theoretical perspective** (Benington & Hartley, 2019; Benington & Moore, 2011; Moore, 1995, 2013; Williams & Shearer, 2011). Public value was first operationalised and applied in the UK context by the Cabinet Office in 2002 (Kelly & Muers, 2002; Kelly, Mulgan, & Muers, 2002), when Table 1.1 was produced to contrast its characteristics with those of traditional Public Administration and New Public Management.

Stoker (2006) argued traditional public administration and new public management sat 'uncomfortably' with networked governance and that Public Value Management was the paradigm most suited to the form of networked governance that was also emerging over the New Labour years. Networked governance (and operations) is clearly appropriate in the context of emergency services where effective collaborations are crucial. Although the Coalition Government of David Cameron and the 2012 National Framework attempted to introduce marketisation and hybridisation based on the operationalisation of New Public Management principles (Cabinet Office, 2011, 2012), these had only a very marginal impact on fire and rescue services, where opportunities for local and national outsourcing were extremely limited. The NAO (2015) and PAC (2016) reports, the Policing and Crime

Table 1.1. Public Administration, New Public Management and Public Value.

	Traditional Public Management	New Public Management	Public Value
Public interest	Defined by politicians/experts	Aggregation of individual preferences, demonstrated by customer choice	Individual and public preferences (resulting from public deliberation)
Performance objective	Managing inputs	Managing inputs and outputs	Multiple objectives • Service outputs • Satisfaction • Outcomes • Maintaining trust/legitimacy
Dominant model of accountability	Upwards through departments to politicians and through them to Parliament	Upwards through performance contracts; sometimes outwards to customers through market mechanisms	Multiple • Citizens as overseers of government • Customers as users • Taxpayers as funders

Table 1.1. (Continued)

	Traditional Public Management	New Public Management	Public Value
Preferred system for delivery	Hierarchical department or self-regulating profession	Private sector or tightly defined arms-length public agency	Menu of alternatives selected pragmatically (public sector agencies, private companies, JVCs, Community Interest Companies, community groups as well as increasing role for user choice)
Approach to public service ethos	Public sector has monopoly on service ethos, and all public bodies have it.	Sceptical of public sector ethos (leads to inefficiency and empire building) – favours customer service	No one sector has a monopoly on ethos, and no one ethos is always appropriate. As a valuable resource it needs to be carefully managed
Role for public participation	Limited to voting in elections and pressure on elected representatives	Limited – apart from use of customer satisfaction surveys	Crucial – multi-faceted (customers, citizens, key stakeholders)
Goal of managers	Respond to political direction	Meet agreed performance targets	Respond to citizen/user preferences, renew mandate and trust through guaranteeing quality services.

Source: Kelly and Muers (2002).

Act 2017 and the 2018 National Framework all re-prioritised and re-emphasised the need for efficient and effective collaborations and networks in protecting the public. The 2017 Act introduced individual directly elected commissioners whose role is to re-connect the service with communities at the local level. Commissioners are in the process of replacing the fire and rescue authorities, local bodies that include local councillors elected to the local authorities.

Public Value would therefore appear apposite for an emergency service, but it is particularly appropriate since Meynhardt and others demonstrated that public value creation is not limited to public sector organisations but can arise from third sector and private sector organisations, even though it may not be the dominant creation of the latter (Meynhardt, 2009, 2015; Meynhardt & Fröhlich, 2019). Thus, for example, outsourced public services or parts of public services are likely to be creating forms of public and social value as well as private value through profits.

However, in order to adopt and operationalise a public value approach, theoretical reasoning has to be translated into tangible measures of corporate performance in order to facilitate evaluation and public reporting. Talbot (2008) initially suggested a competing values approach, but more recently Noordegraaf (2015) and Douglas and Noordegraaf (2019) have developed the Public Value Scorecard, while Meynhardt and Bäro (2019) have compared the Public Value Scorecard to the Public Value Matrix and the more traditional use of Key Performance Indicators.

The commissioner/provider split of the 2012 framework and the abdication of government responsibility for fire service delivery made clear in the Minister's introduction (DCLG, 2012; Murphy, Ferry, & Glennon, 2019; Murphy, Ferry, Glennon, & Greenhalgh, 2019) might have encouraged the adoption of public agency or even public choice theory at least for some analyses and interpretations. However, the significant inadequacies in public policy, service delivery and public accountability between 2010 and 2015 (NAO, 2015; PAC, 2016); the renewed focus on collaboration and partnership working in the Crime and Policing Act 2017, together with the strategic objectives and (admittedly weak) operational content of the 2018 National Framework, all suggest Public Value as the most appropriate theoretical foundation for analysis and evaluation of the service.

At the start of this chapter we thought it might be helpful to establish some of the underpinning assumptions about Fire and Rescue Services in England that have recently been contested under the UK's Coalition Government between 2010 and 2015. By being explicit about these assumptions we hope to facilitate the readers' understanding of our evaluations in Chapters 3 to 5 and the views and recommendations that flow from our evaluations into suggestions for future research and practice in Chapter 6. The next chapter will, however, set out an evaluative model that has been developed to illustrate how performance regimes or national frameworks are configured and demonstrate how key parts of them inter-relate. The model then helps to inform our later evaluations.

REFERENCES

Benington, J., & Hartley, J. (2019). Public Value as a contested democratic practice. In A. Lindgreen, N. Koenig-Lewis, M. Kitchener, J. Brewer, M. Moore, & T. Meynhardt (Eds.), *Public Value: Deepening, enriching and broadening the theory and practice* (pp. 143–158). Abingdon: Routledge.

Benington, J., & Moore, M. (Eds.). (2011). *Public Value: Theory and practice*. London: Palgrave Macmillan.

Cabinet Office. (2011). *Open public services*. White Paper Cm 8145. London: TSO.

Cabinet Office. (2012). *Open public services*. London: Cabinet Office.

Department of Communities and Local Government. (2012). *Fire and rescue national framework for England*. London: TSO.

Douglas, S., & Noordegraaf, M. (2019). Designing spaces for public value creation: Consolidating conflicting dimensions of public value in the design of public organisations. In A. Lindgreen, N. Koenig-Lewis, M. Kitchener, J. Brewer, M. Moore, & T. Meynhardt (Eds.), *Public Value: Deepening, enriching and broadening the theory and practice* (pp. 54–64). Abingdon: Routledge.

FIRE. (2018, June). UK ranked 34th in resilience to fire. *FIRE, 113*(1409), 14.

Glennon, R., & Murphy, P. (2018). Have we forgotten what accountability means? *Public Sector Focus*, (17), 46–47.

Hackitt, J. (2018). *Building a safer future: Independent review of building regulations and fire safety: Final report*. Cm 9607. London: TSO.

Home Office. (2018). *Fire and rescue national framework for England*. London: TSO.

Hurd, N. (2018). *Announcement of the fire and rescue national framework for England*. London: TSO.

Kelly, G., & Muers, S. (2002). *Creating public value: An analytical framework for public service reform*. London: Cabinet Office Strategy Unit.

Kelly, G., Mulgan, G., & Muers, S. (2002). *Creating Public Value: An analytical framework for public service reform.* London: Cabinet Office Prime Minister's Strategy Unit.

May, T. (2016). *Home Secretary speech on fire reform.* London: Home Office.

Meynhardt, T. (2009). Public value inside: What is public value creation? *International Journal of Public Administration, 32*(3), 192–219.

Meynhardt, T. (2015). Public Value: Turning a conceptual framework into a scorecard. In J. Bryson, B. Crosby, & L. Bloomberg (Eds.), *Public Value and public administration* (pp. 147–169), Washington, DC: Georgetown University Press.

Meynhardt, T., & Bäro, A. (2019). Public Value reporting: Adding value to (non-) financial reporting. In A. Lindgreen, N. Koenig-Lewis, M. Kitchener, J. Brewer, M. Moore, & T. Meynhardt (Eds.), *Public Value: Deepening, enriching and broadening the theory and practice* (pp. 87–108). Abingdon: Routledge.

Meynhardt, T., & Fröhlich, A. (2019). More value awareness for more (public) value: Recognizing *how* and *for whom* value is truly created. In A. Lindgreen, N. Koenig-Lewis, M. Kitchener, J. Brewer, M. Moore & T. Meynhardt (Eds.), *Public value: Deepening, enriching and broadening the theory and practice* (pp. 87–108). Abingdon: Routledge.

Moore, M. (1995). *Creating Public Value: Strategic management in government.* Cambridge, MA: Harvard University Press.

Moore, M. (2013). *Recognizing Public Value.* Cambridge, MA: Harvard University Press.

Moore-Bick, M. (2017). The Grenfell Tower inquiry. Retrieved from https://www.grenfelltowerinquiry.org.uk/. Accessed on July 29, 2019.

Murphy, P. (2019). Inspections reveal lack of support or investment. *FIRE, 114*(1415), 14–15.

Murphy, P., Ferry, L., & Glennon, R. (2019). Police. In P. Murphy, L. Ferry, R. Glennon, & K. Greenhalgh (Eds.), *Public service accountability: Rekindling a debate* (pp. 91–105). Cham: Palgrave Macmillan.

Murphy, P., Ferry, L., Glennon, R., & Greenhalgh, K. (2019). *Public service accountability: Rekindling a debate.* Cham: Palgrave Macmillan.

National Audit Office. (2015). *Financial sustainability of fire and rescue services.* HC 491. London: NAO.

Noordegraaf, M. (2015). *Public management: Performance, professionalism and politics.* London: Palgrave Macmillan.

Public Accounts Committee. (2016). *Financial sustainability of fire and rescue services.* Twenty-third Report of Session 2015–2016. London: TSO.

Stoker, G. (2006). Public value management: A new narrative for networked governance? *The American Review of Public Administration, 36*(1), 41–57.

Talbot, C. (2008). *Measuring Public Value: A competing values approach.* London: The Work Foundation.

Wankhade, P., & Weir, D. (2015). *Police services: Leadership and management perspectives.* Cham: Springer.

Williams, I., & Shearer, H. (2011). Appraising Public Value: Past, present and futures. *Public Administration, 89*(4), 1367–1384.

2

THE GOLD STANDARD: AN EVALUATIVE MODEL

2.1 INTRODUCTION

Performance regimes, periodically assembled into national frameworks, became popular with successive governments in the UK during the New Labour administrations of Tony Blair and Gordon Brown, and have continued to exert influence in many public services since then. In the spirit of 'joined-up government', which formed part of the modernisation agenda of the first New Labour administration, governments attempted to embrace a more strategic approach to policy and delivery of public services (Murphy, 2014).

Ministers set out this strategy in policy documents, supplemented by advice, guidance and sometimes new or proposed regulations on how public agencies should deliver the services – either in conjunction with central government agencies and/or with other stakeholders. Revised arrangements intended to improve accountability, transparency and, ultimately, public assurance have also formed part of this package. Nowhere is this more evident than in Fire and Rescue Services, where five successive national frameworks have been issued since the 2004 Fire and Rescue Services Act (DCLG, 2008, 2012; Home Office, 2018; ODPM, 2004, 2006).

Performance regimes and national frameworks should attempt to bring policy development, service delivery and public assurance into a mutually supportive, coherent and joined-up approach. They are defined as

> *the context, the parameters, the agencies and the relationships operating within the three domains of policy development, service delivery and public assurance in public services or sectors.*
> (Murphy, Lakoma, Hayden, & Glennon, 2018)

This chapter sets out a conceptual model that illustrates how the different parts of the frameworks are configured and interrelate (Murphy & Lakoma, 2018). It then uses the model to examine the three aspects of the post-2017 Crime and Policing Act, which are the subject of subsequent chapters.

The breadth of the legislation affecting Fire and Rescue Services is set out in Table 2.1. In this legislation, there are three strategic legislative requirements that represent key priorities for the leadership and management of fire and rescue services. These form part of the legislation, but clearly are not all of it. Services, and the individual organisations that deliver these services, are required, individually and collectively, to (1) facilitate continuous improvement, (2) provide value for money and (3) deliver more accountable and transparent public assurance arrangements. Together, these requirements have been in place since 1998 and form the basis for evaluating performance frameworks. They cover all locally delivered public services within Local Authorities, Health and Social Care, the Police and Fire and Rescue Services.

Table 2.1. Fire and Rescue Services: Legislative Requirements.

Year	Legislation	Government
1998	The Crime and Disorder Act	'New' Labour
1999	The Local Government Act	
2004	The Fire and Rescue Services Act	
2004	The 2004 Civil Contingencies Act	
2005	Regulatory reform (fire safety) order	
2006	Safeguarding Vulnerable Groups Act	
2010	Equalities Act	
2010	Building Regulations Act	Conservative/Liberal Democrat Coalition
2012	Public Services (Social Value) Act	
2014	Local Audit and Accountability Act	
2015, 1974, 2005	Health and Safety Acts	Conservative
2017	The Policing and Crime Act	

Source: Murphy, Lakoma, Eckersley & Glennon.

The conceptual model described in Figs. 2.1 and 2.2 can be utilised as an analytical tool in order to evaluate how well individual frameworks, or parts of frameworks, cover the relevant areas, or can also be used to evaluate successive versions of frameworks longitudinally against these three requirements. Fig. 2.1 provides specific, practical detail against each of the three domains, and Fig. 2.2 sets those domains in the context of an overarching conceptual framework.

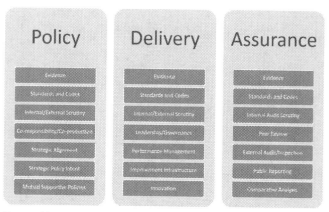

Source: Murphy and Lakoma (2018).

Fig. 2.1. The Three Core Domains of Policy, Delivery and Assurance.

2.2 THE THREE CORE DOMAINS

In order to ensure that national frameworks for performance measurement, management and monitoring are comprehensive and effective, they include activity in the following three interconnected 'domains' of policy, delivery and assurance:

- **policy or policy development** – this determines the objectives of any policy, whether national, regional or local. It also identifies what the parameters to its development are, and whether delivery is feasible and realistic

- **service delivery** – this determines how the service is to be delivered and ideally how its delivery is to be optimised, continually improved, sustained, innovated and constructively monitored, and

- **public assurance or regulation** – this demonstrates how the public is to be provided with reassurance that the money taken from them to finance the policy prescriptions and the strategic and operational delivery of the service is justified and provides value for money.

Joined-up policy development and policy making is particularly important in services (such as the emergency services) that have mutually interdependent responsibilities to the public at national, regional and local community levels (Kozuch & Sienkiewicz-Malyjurek, 2014; Sienkiewicz-Malyjurek, 2017). Efficient and effective service delivery is also equally interdependent at local, regional and national levels. Finally, the objectives of the assurance and regulatory arrangements need to transcend all emergency services to address wider community or public goals and objectives such

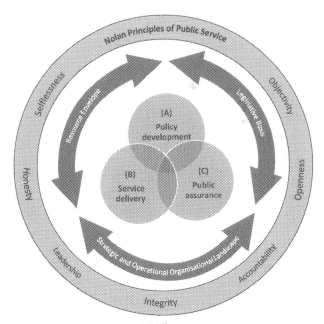

Source: Murphy and Lakoma (2018).

Fig. 2.2. National Frameworks: A Comprehensive Model.

as public safety and security, rather than prioritise narrower individual organisational goals and objectives.

These three inter-connected domains, which are illustrated in more detail in Fig. 2.2, clearly have areas of overlap and some of their individual aspects or components are common to more than one domain. For example, in fire and rescue all three domains draw on many common elements of a (more or less robust and quality assured) evidence base (see Chapter 3). In addition, some aspects are specific to an individual domain, such as a strategic policy intent, performance management or external audit and inspection. These three core domains also inter-relate with the three broader parameters that make up the first circle that surrounds them, namely resource availability, authorising legislation and the organisational landscape. At the same time, all aspects and activities in both the core domain and the parameters need to adhere to the principles, values and behavioural norms in the outer circle, which are the values and behaviours by which public service is conducted in the UK.

2.3 THE NOLAN PRINCIPLES: VALUES AND BEHAVIOURS

Two definitive overarching assumptions drive any public service framework; these are the public interest, and the values and principles that are enshrined within public service. In the UK, this is currently relatively simple to identify since anyone who works as a public office holder or a direct or indirect employee of the public sector must adhere to the seven principles of public life known as the 'Nolan Principles' (Committee on Standards in Public Life, 1995). These values are selflessness, integrity, objectivity, accountability, openness, honesty and leadership. They are shown in Fig. 2.2 as the large outer circle and defined in Table 2.2. In developing any

Table 2.2. The Nolan Principles.

Standard	Description
1. Selflessness	Holders of public office should act solely in terms of the public interest.
2. Integrity	Holders of public office must avoid placing themselves under any obligation to people or organisations that might try inappropriately to influence them in their work. They should not act or take decisions in order to gain financial or other material benefits for themselves, their family or their friends. They must declare and resolve any interests and relationships.
3. Objectivity	Holders of public office must act and take decisions impartially, fairly and on merit, using the best evidence and without discrimination or bias.
4. Accountability	Holders of public office are accountable to the public for their decisions and actions and must submit themselves to the scrutiny necessary to ensure this.
5. Openness	Holders of public office should act and take decisions in an open and transparent manner. Information should not be withheld from the public unless there are clear and lawful reasons for so doing.
6. Honesty	Holders of public office should be truthful.
7. Leadership	Holders of public office should exhibit these principles in their own behaviour. They should actively promote and robustly support the principles and be willing to challenge poor behaviour wherever it occurs.

Source: Committee on Standards in Public Life (1995. p. 1).

policy initiatives or arrangements for service delivery, ministers, legislators and officials must adhere to and promote these principles in their work. The principles operate throughout any public activity, and in any public service context. Public service principles are not unique to the UK, but the Nolan Principles are universal to UK public services.

In addition to these values and the core domains, there are a number of situational or contextual constraints that act as the strategic parameters for the development of service frameworks and other policy/service/assurance regimes. Most national policy documents and frameworks (for example, the five National Frameworks for Fire and Rescue Services published since 2004 (DCLG, 2008, 2012; Home Office, 2018; ODPM, 2004, 2006)) begin by attempting to cover these situational issues and contextual constraints. In effect, they serve to 'set the scene' for any proposals that follow in the main body of the policy or framework. In addition to the timescales (short, medium and long term) that any framework is expected to cover, they generally include three key contextual components that are represented as the second inner circle in Fig. 2.2. These are the resource envelopes deemed to be available; the legislative basis that provides the authority and legitimacy for the proposals; and the current or revised strategic and operational organisational landscape within which the service operates. They are set out in more detail in the following section.

2.4 THE RESOURCE ENVELOPE

Between 2010 and 2019, three Conservative-led administrations implemented a macro-economic strategy of severe deficit reduction, more generally known as 'austerity' (Atkinson, 2015; Blyth, 2013; O'Hara, 2015; Schui, 2015). This policy response has been exemplified by successive reductions in public expenditure on public services – whether these services are delivered directly by central government and their agencies, or more locally by local government, the NHS, the Police or the Fire and Rescue Services. As the Coalition's programme for government stated in 2010:

> *The deficit reduction programme takes precedence over any of the other measures in this agreement, and the speed of implementation of any measures that have a cost to the public finances will depend on decisions to be made in the Comprehensive Spending Review.* (HMG, 2010, p. 35)

Periodic macro-economic, medium-term spending reviews were initiated by the first New Labour administration but were later embraced by successors of all political persuasions (Ferry & Eckersley, 2011). Although the form and extent of reductions in financial support from central government may have varied, and individual services may have experienced different temporal and geographic impacts, successive governments since 2010 instituted continuous reductions in the aggregate of public expenditure for public services through a series of Spending Reviews and associated financial statements (HMT, 1998, 2010, 2013, 2015, 2017, 2018; HMT/DWP, 2013). Thus, what Whitehall often refers to as the 'resource envelope' for public services generally, and for Fire and Rescue Services in particular, has been reducing substantially in real terms (HMICFRS, 2019; Murphy, 2019; NAO, 2015). Fire and Rescue Services also raise revenue locally through a council tax precept and there are some minor services or activities for which they may be able to level charges or fees, e.g. the hiring of its apparatus or copies of plans and licenses. Council tax rises have, however, effectively been capped for some time and the punitive 'gearing' system for increasing this ensures that large rises are impractical (Bandy, 2015). This has had a significant effect on both local government and fire services. The National Audit Office estimated that stand-alone fire authorities experienced an average of 17% in real terms reduction in spending power from 2010/11 to 2015/16 (NAO, 2015). In practice, therefore, resource envelopes have been significantly restricted, limiting the activities of policy development, service delivery and public assurance functions for fire and rescue services since 2010.

2.5 THE LEGISLATIVE BASE AND AN ANALYTICAL LENS

The New Labour administration of 1997–2001 introduced two new statutory requirements on public services and redefined the way that a third, 'value for money', was to be determined. The first was to re-introduce the concept of multiple organisations having responsibility for tackling long-term deep-rooted social, economic and environmental problems. These included issues that had clearly been adversely affecting local communities for some time and were proving increasingly problematic, despite government policy and action to mitigate their impact. In academic and practitioner literature they had become known as 'wicked' issues or problems (Rittel & Webber, 1973).

Wicked issues are not amenable to single agency action (whether government or non-government) but require concerted and co-ordinated action on the part of multiple agencies to address them. The first statutory application of multiple organisational responsibility in the New Labour era was the 1998 Crime and Disorder Act, which established Crime and Disorder Reduction Partnerships in every local authority area of the UK (Phillips, Jacobson, Prime, Carter,

& Considine, 2002). The police and local authorities were the primary responsible agencies but Fire and Rescue Services have also been active participants in these partnerships since their inception; more recently these partnerships have become known as Community Safety Partnerships.

The second innovation, which later became known as the 'improvement agenda' (DETR, 1998), was to require public bodies to facilitate continuous improvement across all of their services and activities, rather than just be subject to the local political dictates of their governing boards or authorities. This was first introduced in the Local Government Act 1999, which *inter alia* required local authorities to seek to achieve 'Best Value'. Best Value also changed the obligation on public services to achieve value for money, in that value for money was henceforth to be assessed according to the 3 'e's of economy, efficiency and effectiveness by which they commissioned and delivered services and activities to the public (DETR, 1998). The two new concepts, along with the revised notion of Best Value, were translated into statutory requirements that are still extant at the time of writing, despite prophesies of their demise (Glennon, 2017). For a short time under Gordon Brown's administration (2007–2010), 'equality' and 'sustainability' were added to the 3 'e's but subsequent governments have reverted in practice to the 3 'e's.

In developing national policy for public service improvement, the New Labour administrations attempted to integrate the development and implementation of central government policy into local delivery organisations, with a mechanism called Public Service Agreements, which also included delivery targets for individual Whitehall departments (HMT, 1998). These were initially linked to the Spending Reviews that provided successive rounds of central government funding via Departmental Expenditure Limits to individual Whitehall departments. In effect the central government core (comprising HMT, the Cabinet Office and the Number 10 Strategy Unit) negotiated increasingly sophisticated delivery targets (which might be input, output or increasingly outcome-based targets) with individual 'delivery' or spending ministries (the Departments of Health, Transport, Education, etc) in exchange for Treasury funding. This Public Service Agreement system rapidly developed into an approach that determined individual and multi-department objectives and targets.

This new 'joined-up' policy approach was complemented by a parallel attempt across Whitehall departments to link up policy and delivery. Government sought to achieve this through the development of co-production and co-delivery of public services with their main external delivery agents, including local authorities, the police, the NHS and non-departmental public bodies (Cabinet Office, 1999; HMG, 1998). The commitment and obligation to public consultation was one of the original four 'C's of Best Value, namely Compare, Consult, Compete and Challenge (DETR, 1998), through which local authorities needed to develop their strategies and policies and which sat alongside the 3 'E's for assessing service delivery. Local delivery was shaped by Local Public Service Agreements and successive rounds of Local Area Agreements (LAAs), which were predicated on multi-agency working at the local community levels. Although the Conservative-led Coalition of 2010–2015 formally abandoned LAAs, the requirement for multi-agency collaboration among local delivery organisation was enshrined in later legislation such as the 2012 Health and Social Care Act, which established Health and Wellbeing Boards, and more latterly the 2017 Crime and Policing Act.

This more collective and collaborative approach to policy development and public service delivery was also complemented by a system of internal and external audit, and the measurement and monitoring of performance intended to ensure that costs were reduced and the quality of services improved (Ashworth, Boyne, & Entwistle, 2010; Martin, 2006). By creating and strengthening external inspection, auditing, regulation and assurance bodies, ministers sought to support this improvement agenda and also provide greater accountability and transparency of public services. This aimed to assure the government and the public about public service performance and financial conformance, at the same time as facilitating, driving and encouraging improvement (Ashworth et al., 2010; Davis & Martin, 2008).

New Labour placed these initiatives, and the attempt to generate a more mutually supportive and coherent programme of improvement, at the heart of their programme of Public Service Reforms. Essentially, these were multifaceted baskets of changes to policy development, service delivery and public assurance. They operated at national and local levels under the New Labour administrations, although they also covered the devolved administrations for Scotland, Wales and Northern Ireland and often had regional components within England (Cabinet Office/DTLR, 2002; House of Commons Library, 2003). The statutory obligation to deliver continuous improvement has remained throughout the UK, although since 2010 it has been given greater prominence in the devolved administrative areas than in England. For example, as indicated in the quote from the Coalition's programme for government in 2010, successive UK governments have consistently emphasised the austerity programme over the improvement agenda although both remain statutory obligations (Glennon, 2017). In contrast, public service delivery and improvement remained a significant feature of the strategic intent of the devolved governments in Scotland and Wales. Recent studies have examined these two contrasting strategies in the case of Fire and Rescue Services

(Murphy, Lakoma, Greenhalgh, & Taylor, 2019; Taylor, Murphy, & Greenhalgh, 2018), and suggested that the Scottish approach has been the more successful.

2.6 THE ORGANISATIONAL LANDSCAPE

The period between 2004 and 2017 saw widespread significant changes in the organisational landscape of Fire and Rescue Services in England (Murphy, Wankhade, & Lakoma, 2019). The number of fire authorities or services remained relatively constant but for a few horizontal amalgamations, but New Labour's performance management and improvement infrastructure, as well as its arrangements for public assurance, were washed away by the incoming Conservative and Liberal Democrat Coalition Government. In particular, its response to the 2008–2010 recession centred on policies of austerity localism (Lowndes & Pratchett, 2012) and sector-led improvement in locally delivered public services (Murphy & Jones, 2016).

Between July and September 2010, the incoming Coalition Government announced that it would abolish the Audit Commission, abandon Comprehensive Area Assessment, terminate all commission inspections, decommission LAAs and transfer the external audit of public bodies to private sector audit firms (Murphy, 2014). The Audit Commission was formally closed on 31 March 2015, although in reality it had only a skeleton staff and vastly reduced capacity to operate from 2012 onwards. The Local Government Association had closed the Improvement and Development Agency and its Leadership Centre while the Fire Service College and the Emergency Planning Colleges were sold to Capita and Serco, respectively. (Capita and Serco are international business process outsourcing and services companies, and both firms rely heavily on public sector contracts.) The new government issued a new national framework (DCLG, 2012) and adopted a policy approach that had remarkable similarities to the 'benign neglect' of the pre-New Labour Home Office (Murphy & Greenhalgh, 2013; Raynsford, 2016).

The baleful regime at the Department of Communities and Local Government under Eric Pickles resulted, five years later, in a series of reports that castigated the service and the sector for poor leadership, lack of knowledge and information, inadequate performance management, loss of accountability and transparency and failure to protect the public as much as it could and should have done (Ferry & Murphy, 2015; Murphy, 2015; NAO, 2015; PAC, 2016); this was more a case of malign neglect than benign. As a result, policy responsibility was passed back to the Home Office and Theresa May expedited a series of reforms based on her 2010–2015 programme of reforms for the police.

As a consequence of implementation of the 2012 National Framework, co-production and collective responsibility between government and the fire services in policy development had shifted to organisational, hierarchical responsibility through Fire Authorities. Local accountability too was ostensibly opened up to citizens, some of whom were anticipated to emerge as 'armchair auditors' to ensure public assurance (DCLG, 2012; Ferry, Eckersley, & Zakaria, 2015; Pickles, 2011). This was in parallel with Fire Authorities in theory having more freedom and flexibility but in practice being heavily constrained by spending cuts and restrictions on raising local revenue.

The process for developing the 2018 framework under the Home Office was the antithesis of open, consensual, joined-up, evidence-based policy making. Lip service was paid to statutory obligations such as public consultations, through incredibly short consultation timescales. All responses came from either Police and Crime Commissioners or from the Fire and Rescue sector, and in reality, the public's view played little part. The inadequacy of the evidence base had been further confirmed by the Hackitt Review (Hackitt, 2018) and whilst a new central body for standards, codes and regulations and a dedicated website for information had been promised, both of these were in the early stages of development at that time.

The organisational landscape of service delivery in England became more complex with the introduction of discretionary Police, Fire and Crime Commissioners. Unlike Scotland or Northern Ireland, which have single services answerable to the devolved administration (when not suspended in Northern Ireland), and London and Greater Manchester, which have directly elected mayors, the remainder of England has legacy county, combined or metropolitan fire authorities, or one or other Police Fire and Crime Commissioner models. The previous momentum to encourage delivery at larger geographical units, and hence achieve economies of scale, has changed direction in England, although not in Scotland (Murphy, Lakoma, et al., 2019; Murphy, Wankhade, et al., 2019; Taylor et al., 2018). Most, if not all, English Fire and Rescue Services are actively pursuing collaborations with the police, particularly around back office functions such as procurement and estates strategy. This is a result of the statutory obligation for collaboration agreements anticipated by Chapter 1 of the Policing and Crime Act 2017. It remains to be seen whether pressures to amalgamate will re-emerge or disappear as there are clearly still economies of scale, organisational efficiencies and consequent resilience of larger services to capture.

Finally, in terms of public assurance, accountability and transparency, but also potentially in terms of service improvement, the role and responsibilities of HMICFRS appears increasingly significant. For HMICFRS to be effective it will need a more robust evidence base than is currently available to the sector. It will also need to be strategically positioned in the organisational landscape of the sector. Key stakeholders such as the emerging Standards Board will need to be effectively managed, and the revised Building Regulations and the internal and external public auditing arrangements will need to be configured so as to be mutually beneficial. This will require satisfactory relationships with key stakeholders in the policy development and service delivery domains, as well as more harmonious relationships with the legislators and resource providers. The lack or inadequacy of any of these factors could prove seriously detrimental to public assurance, and it is not yet clear how well HMICFRS will be able to manage these tensions. The antecedents and initial development of HMICFRS will be examined in more detail in Chapter 5.

REFERENCES

Ashworth, R. E., Boyne, G. A., & Entwistle, T. (2010). *Public service improvement: Theories and evidence*. Oxford: Oxford University Press.

Atkinson, A. B. (2015). *Inequality: What can be done?* Cambridge, MA: Harvard University Press.

Bandy, G. (2015). *Financial management and accounting in the public sector* (2nd ed.). Abingdon: Routledge.

Blyth, M. (2013). *Austerity: The history of a dangerous idea*. Oxford: Oxford University Press.

Cabinet Office. (1999). *Modernising government Cm 4310*. London: TSO.

Cabinet Office/DTLR. (2002). *Your region, your choice revitalising the English regions Cm 5511*. London: TSO.

Committee on Standards in Public Life. (1995). *Standards in public life: First report of the committee on standards in public life*. London: TSO.

Davis, H., & Martin, S. J. (2008). *Public services inspection in the UK*. London: Jessica Kingsley.

Department of Communities and Local Government. (2008). *Fire and rescue service national framework 2008–11*. Wetherby: DCLG.

Department of Communities and Local Government. (2012). *Fire and rescue national framework for England*. London: DCLG/TSO.

Department of the Environment Transport and Regions. (1998). *Modernising local government – Improving local services through best value*. London: TSO.

Ferry, L., & Eckersley, P. (2011). Budgeting and governing for deficit reduction in the UK public sector: Act one 'the comprehensive spending review'. *The Journal of Finance and Management in Public Services*, 10(1), 14–23.

Ferry, L., Eckersley, P., & Zakaria, Z. (2015). Accountability and transparency in English local government: Moving from 'matching parts' to 'awkward couple'? *Financial Accountability and Management*, 31(3), 345–361.

Ferry, L., & Murphy, P. (2015). Financial sustainability, accountability and transparency across local public service bodies in England under austerity. Report to National Audit Office (NAO). Nottingham: NTU.

Glennon, R. (2017). *The 'death of improvement': An exploration of the legacy of performance and service improvement reform in English Local Authorities 1997–2017*. Ph.D. thesis, Loughborough University, Loughborough.

Hackitt, J. (2018). *Building a safer future – Independent review of building regulations and fire safety: Final report.* London: Ministry of Housing, Communities and Local Government.

HM Government. (2010). *The coalition: Our programme for government. Freedom, fairness and responsibility.* London: TSO and Cabinet Office.

HM Inspectorate of Constabulary and Fire & Rescue Services. (2019). *Fire and rescue inspections 2018/19 summary of findings from Tranche 2.* London: HMICFRS.

HM Treasury. (1998). *Modern public services for Britain: Investing in reform comprehensive spending review: New public spending plans 1999–2002 July 1998.* Cm 4011. London: TSO.

HM Treasury. (2010). *Spending review 2010.* Cm 7942. London: TSO.

HM Treasury. (2013). *Spending round 2013.* Cm 8639. London: TSO.

HM Treasury. (2015). *The Spending review and autumn statement 2015.* Cm 9162. London: TSO.

HM Treasury. (2017). *HM Treasury single departmental plan.* London: TSO.

HM Treasury. (2018). *Budget 2018. HC. 1629 2018–19.* London: TSO.

HM Treasury, Department for Work and Pensions, HM Revenues and Customs and the Rt Hon George Osborne. (2013). *Autumn statement 2013.* Cm8747. London: TSO.

Home Office. (2018). *Fire and rescue national framework for England.* London: Home Office.

House of Commons Library. (2003). *An introduction to devolution in the UK*. Research Paper 03/84 published 17th November 2003. London: House of Commons Library.

Kozuch, B., & Sienkiewicz-Malyjurek, K. (2014). New requirements for managers of public safety management systems. *Procedia: Social and Behavioural Sciences, 149*, 472–478.

Lowndes, V., & Pratchett, L. (2012). Local governance under the coalition government: austerity, localism and the big society. *Local Government Studies, 38*(1), 21–40.

Martin, S. (Ed.). (2006). *Public service improvement: Policies, progress and prospects*. New York, NY: Routledge.

Murphy, P. (2014). The development of the strategic state and the performance management of local authorities in England. In P. Joyce & A. Drumaux (Eds.), *Strategic management in public organizations: European practices and perspectives* (pp. 243–255). Abingdon: Routledge.

Murphy, P. (2015). *Briefing note on 'financial sustainability of fire and rescue services-value for money report' for the National Audit Office*. London: NAO.

Murphy, P., & Jones, M. (2016). Building the next model for intervention and turnaround in poorly performing local authorities in England. *Local Government Studies, 42*(5), 698–716.

Murphy, P. (2019). Inspections reveal lack of support or investment. *FIRE, 114*(1415), 14–15.

Murphy, P., & Greenhalgh, K., (2013). Performance management in fire and rescue services. *Public Money & Management, 33*(3), 225–232.

Murphy, P., & Lakoma, K. (2018). Shifting tectonic plates: Changes to the strategic and operational landscape of the emergency services in the UK. In *Fire related research and developments conference (RE18)*, West Midlands Fire & Rescue Service Headquarters, Birmingham.

Murphy, P., Lakoma, K., Greenhalgh, K., & Taylor, L. (2019). A comparative appraisal of recent and proposed changes to the fire and rescue services in England and Scotland. In P. Wankhade, L. McCann, & P. Murphy (Eds.), *Critical perspectives on the management and organization of emergency services*. Routledge critical studies in public management. Abingdon: Routledge.

Murphy, P., Lakoma, K., Hayden, J., & Glennon, R. (2018). Do the pieces of the jigsaw fit? Evaluating the national framework for fire and rescue services in England. In *Fire related research and developments conference (RE18)*, West Midlands Fire & Rescue Service Headquarters, Birmingham.

Murphy, P., Wankhade, P., & Lakoma, K. (2019). The strategic and operational landscape of emergency services in the UK. *International Journal of Emergency Services*. Available at https://doi.org/10.1108/IJES-12-2018-0062.

National Audit Office. (2015). *Department for Communities and Local Government: Financial sustainability of fire and rescue services*. London: NAO.

O'Hara, M. (2015). *Austerity bites: A journey to the sharp end of cuts in the UK*. Bristol: Policy Press.

Office of the Deputy Prime Minister. (2004). *The fire and rescue service national framework 2004/05*. London: TSO.

Office of the Deputy Prime Minister. (2006). *The fire and rescue service national framework 2006/07*. London: TSO.

Phillips, C., Jacobson, J., Prime, R., Carter, M., & Considine, M. (2002). Crime and disorder reduction partnerships: Round one progress. Police research series (151). Home Office, Policing and Reducing Crime Unit, London.

Pickles, E. (2011). Armchair auditors are here to stay. DCLG. Retrieved from http://www.communities.gov.uk/news/localgovernment/1941304. Accessed on July 18, 2019.

Public Accounts Committee. (2016). *Financial sustainability of fire and rescue services*. Twenty-third report of session 2015–16. London: TSO.

Raynsford, N. (2016). *Substance not spin: An insiders view of success and failure in government*. Bristol: Policy Press.

Rittel, H., & Webber, M. (1973). Dilemmas in a general theory of planning. *Policy Sciences*, 4(2), 155–169.

Schui, F. (2015). *Austerity: The great failure*. New Haven, CT: Yale University Press.

Sienkiewicz-Malyjurek, K. (2017). *Inter-organisational collaboration in the public safety management system*. Warsaw: Scholar Publishing House.

Taylor, L., Murphy, P., & Greenhalgh, K. (2018). Scottish fire and rescue services reform 2010–2015. In P. Murphy & K. Greenhalgh (Eds.), *Fire and rescue services: Leadership and management perspectives* (pp. 191–205). London: Springer.

3

A SINKING PLATFORM:
THE DATA DILEMMA

*I want 2017 to be a big year for fire and rescue. I
want this to be the year when real change happens...
And to support greater transparency and to
encourage greater accountability I will also be
creating a new website, operational this year, to
mirror what we see on www.police.uk. This website
will hold a range of information, all in one place,
about the fire and rescue service. This will include
data which helps the public to assess the performance
of their local service as well as information about
chief officer pay, expenditure, accounts, efficiency
plans and workforce composition.*
(Rt Hon Brandon Lewis Minister for Policing and the
Fire Service. 7 February 2017)

*Data needs to improve. We are concerned about the
absence of consistent, comparable and good quality
data available within each fire and rescue service and
across services in England. The lack of data makes it
hard for services to be sure they are providing the*

> *right support to the public. This problem, combined*
> *with the absence of existing national standards, has*
> *resulted in local variations in almost every aspect of*
> *what each fire and rescue service does. The public*
> *can't always be sure they will receive the same quality*
> *of support from fire and rescue services or*
> *understand the justification for variations between*
> *areas. This situation needs to improve.*
>
> (HMICFRS December 2018a, p. 20)

3.1 INTRODUCTION

There is no shortage of reliable witnesses to contend that the scope, nature, content and aggregate of evidence available to measure, manage and monitor fire and rescue services and inform local and national policy makers, the deliverers of fire and rescue services and the internal and external assurance community, in England and Wales is demonstrably deficient (HMICFRS, 2019; Murphy & Ferry, 2018; NAO, 2015).

This chapter will provide a review of the evidence base that is available for policy development (at local and national levels); the management and monitoring of service delivery; and the public assurance regime for fire and rescue services. However, the purpose of our analysis will not only be to ascertain whether it is inadequate or fit for purpose but also to try to identify which parts or areas of the collective evidence base are inadequate or in some cases completely missing. Therefore, we will evaluate the data and intelligence that form part of the performance management regime alongside the adequacy of the tools, techniques and analytical systems and models available to interrogate, analyse and interpret it.

3.1.1 The Role of Evidence in Fire and Rescue Services

Our model in Chapter 2 clearly shows that evidence is essential to all three domains of policy, delivery and assurance. Some pieces of evidence may be required in all three domains, whereas others might just be needed in one or two. It is therefore helpful to view the requirements as a Venn diagram, with some information needed for policy formulation, some for service delivery, some for public assurance, and some for all three. However, in a small sector or community of interest such as fire and rescue it is more feasible for all performance data (other than data that must remain confidential) to be shared across all three domains (Fig. 3.1).

This leads us to our second distinction. In the generic model, we argue that it is helpful to distinguish between the strategic and operational landscape at the organisational level. Similarly, it is helpful to differentiate and investigate which data and information (and the quality, quantity and sophistication of interrogation and interpretation) are available to inform decision making at the **operational level** (in all three domains), and which may be inadequate or missing at the **strategic level**.

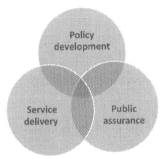

Fig. 3.1. The Policy, Delivery and Assurance Domains.

Finally, it is helpful to make one further analytical distinction in order to identify which of the five broad functional areas of fire and rescue operations are currently well served by evidence, information and interpretive tools and which parts are less well served. These five areas, which we believe will be recognisable to policy makers, practitioners and academics alike in the fire and rescue community, are:

- Response to incidents

- Control rooms

- Prevention and protective services

- Corporate and Management services

- Multi-Agency Partnerships and Collaborations

With these analytical distinctions now clear, we are now better placed to compare this evidence base and its application to other public services and sectors. This helps to ascertain whether there are any transferable lessons to be learnt from evidential bases being deployed, developed and improved in other services or sectors in the UK. Similarly, are there any lessons to be learnt from elsewhere? After all, almost every country in the world has some kind of fire and rescue service. The recent Hackitt Report (2018) and the Global Resilience Index (FIRE, 2018) quoted in Chapter 1 suggest that we can learn such lessons. The former revealed multiple inadequacies in England's Building Regulation system and its enforcement arrangements, including the adequacy of information available, whereas the latter ranked the UK 34th in the world for fire resilience, its lowest historical ranking. Commenting on the anticipated implications of the Hackitt review, Tom Roche the Senior Consultant for International Codes and Standards at FM Global, said:

Hackitt's report focusses heavily on high rise residential buildings. No doubt this is an important area post-Grenfell. However, Grenfell exposed multiple failings across the UK's fire safety systems that were not just specific to high-rise buildings. When it comes to fire safety, we need the same level of rigour to be applied to all buildings, including homes, schools, hospitals, and workplaces, many of which are low rise buildings.

In terms of both policy and delivery, the UK has been a pioneer and international leader in the development of fire and rescue services. This has been based on a long attachment and strong adherence to evidence at both the local and national levels. Standards and practices have been predominantly developed by policy makers in close collaboration with practitioners and any changes have traditionally needed robust justification (Ewen, 2010; Murphy & Greenhalgh, 2018).

In terms of public assurance, however, the quality and consistency of standards deteriorated to such an extent that the government proposed establishing a professional standards body in 2017, and the independently chaired Fire Standards Board began operating two years later. In establishing the board, the National Fire Chiefs' Council (NFCC) stated that 'consistency, learning from incidents and developing fit-for-purpose fire and rescue services standards' would be the 'key focus' of the board. It would oversee FRS's professional standards, support 'continuous improvement' of services, and have responsibility for a 'high-quality, useable framework of professional standards focused on achieving positive outcomes'. Thus it would be concerned with service performance standards as well as professional standards (NFCC, 2018a, 2018b). Its business case provided a very useful update on the 'key gaps' in the current evidence land-scape (NFCC, 2018b), and it appointed an independent Chair and Vice Chair in January 2019.

Evidence is also a key factor in investigating major incidents, particularly fire-related fatalities that require a formal investigation. Depending on the circumstances, this may be local in nature, but more widespread or major incidents often lead to a public inquiry. There is little doubt that the possibility of a coroner's court, a judicial review or a public inquiry interested in facts, evidence and apportioning responsibility has been a strong historical influence on the development of the fire service and the collection and use of evidence (Murphy & Greenhalgh, 2018, p. 2). This focus on the importance of robust data and evidence may or may not still be true at the local level, but as HMICFRS (2018a) has pointed out, national actors appear to be less concerned about such matters.

3.2 RESPONDING TO INCIDENTS AND CALLOUTS

We now examine the five functional areas of fire and rescue services, from both local and national perspectives and operational and strategic standpoints. We begin with the activity that is most strongly associated with fire services: namely, their response to calls for the service to attend incidents and emergencies. How good is the evidence base that local services use to underpin their response, and how good is the collective evidence base when needing to respond to incidents in neighbouring areas, regional or national emergencies? Is it good enough to facilitate and improve policy, practice and public assurance?

Efficient and effective operational response to emergencies has historically and internationally been the primary thing that the public care most about from fire and rescue services. Grenfell Tower demonstrated how important effective fire and rescue services are in keeping the public safe in the UK – and a recent survey found that the British public held these services consistently in high regard and felt that they would respond effectively if required (HMICFRS, 2018a). The inspectorate's first round of reports into FRSs confirmed that staff are highly skilled, have access to a range of equipment and that most of the 30 services they inspected were 'good' at responding to emergencies (HMICFRS, 2018a, 2019).

In the individual service reports and the two summary reports published by HMICFRS by Summer 2019, a direct question (No 1.4) asks how effective the FRS is at responding to fires and other emergencies. Together with questions on understanding risk, prevention, protection and responding to national risks, it forms the inspectorate's assessment of each service's 'effectiveness'. Question 1.4 is accompanied by eight descriptors, which provide an indication of the expected levels of performance consistent with each of four gradings: outstanding; good; requires improvement; and inadequate.

A judgement of good is the 'expected' graded judgement. Good is based on policy, practice or performance that meets pre-defined grading criteria that are informed by relevant national operational guidance or standards. If the policy, practice or performance exceeds what is expected for good, a graded judgement of outstanding may be awarded (HMICFRS, 2018b). In terms of question 1.4 a service is outstanding if it is

> 'at the forefront of developing, sharing and
> influencing best practice in the response to fire and
> other emergencies; ...and ...has established a culture

> *of continuous improvement with outstanding*
> *examples of sustained service development and*
> *improvement that translate into better service for the*
> *public'.*
>
>   (HMICFRS, 2018b, p.3 'Graded judgements')

In total, 20 services scored 'good' for effectiveness overall, and 19 of these were judged 'good' for question 1.4. In all bar two of these cases, the inspectorate identified specific areas for improvements. Only one (the West Midlands) scored 'outstanding' for this question.

In its summary reports the inspectorate reported that after a decade of localism there is a marked difference *inter alia* in how services determine and record their response standards (HMICFRS, 2018b, 2019).

> *in some services firefighters were working with out of*
> *date or inaccurate information, or were unable*
> *readily and efficiently to access this information due*
> *to poor technology.*
>
>   (HMICFRS, 2019, p. 5)

At first, HMICFRS only anticipated publishing its first 'State of Fire and Rescue' report after inspecting every FRS in England; however, the organisation was sufficiently concerned by its initial findings to single out two emerging issues for immediate attention. First, services need to be more consistent in the way they define risk, calculate and communicate response standards; and second, the sector as a whole was in need of more support in order to change and modernise. The former reflects wider concerns across the sector about the evidence base and methodologies that would help to update Integrated Risk Management Plans (Murphy, Ferry, Glennon, & Greenhalgh, 2019; Murphy, Lakoma, & Toothill, 2019). The latter reflects wider concerns about the long-term financial resilience of services and the adequacy of statements of assurance (Spencer, Hayden, Murphy, & Glennon, 2019). Notably, FRSs are required by statute to publish both of these documents.

Moreover, both concerns highlight a lack of consistency in definitions, data collection methods and analysis across the country, which leads to a national picture that is even more unclear and inadequate. Properly assured, high-quality data are vital to national policy making and national resilience. Effective tools, systems and processes to capture, interrogate and interpret raw data and make it accessible to policy developers, service deliverers, and intelligible to the public are essential to ensure that policies and public services are well designed, achieving their objectives and accountable to taxpayers (Murphy & Glennon, 2018). Yet, as the National Audit Office (2015) and the Public Accounts Committee (2016) found, the evidence base provided to fire and rescue services is neither sufficiently comprehensive nor comprehensible (Murphy, Ferry, et al., 2019). Datasets are partial, contradictory and deteriorating, and the processes used for compiling them are no longer fit for purpose – as former prime minister Theresa May acknowledged in 2016 (May, 2016).

One key way in which datasets can improve responses to emergencies and callouts is through a better assessment of fire risks. These comprise both risks to people (individuals and communities) and risks to buildings, properties and premises. The Home Office issues guidance on the assessment of risks to individual types of land, buildings or property, although this advice is not comprehensive and much of it dates from the mid-2000s. Nonetheless, we can assess risks to people and places and superimpose them on a geographical area to inform service configuration. Constructing an appropriate evidence base to facilitate an area-wide IRMP in this way proved extremely difficult, time-consuming and complicated when one author was invited by Nottingham-shire FRS to assist with its Fire Cover Review in 2010 (Murphy, Greenhalgh, & Parkin, 2012). However, the adequacy of the IRMP and the methodology and data that underpinned the process were relatively good compared to other FRSs.

At that time, the vast majority of services were using the fire service emergency cover toolkit (FSET), and this provided some consistency in terms of definitions, standards and reporting. By 2019, however, few services were using the FSET, although IRMPs continue to be the foundation of ser-vice assessment and configuration of fire services. The IRMP process has not been questioned or systematically investi-gated; it has formed part of the last three national frameworks (DCLG, 2008, 2012; Home Office, 2019). Assessing the adequacy of these plans was not part of the scope of the recent HMICFRS inspections, but a recent (admittedly small) survey of contemporary plans suggests that it is likely to be just as difficult to update IRMPs today as it was in 2010 (Murphy, Lakoma, et al., 2019).

Another national dataset in need of urgent review and recalibration is the financial data, both in terms of response but also more generally. A lack of central support and infra-structure meant it became impossible to be assured that fire services were providing value for money (Murphy, Ferry, et al., 2019; NAO, 2015; PAC, 2016). Previously, 'economic cost of fire' statistics calculated the overall impact of fires in England and Wales on the economy. They included the esti-mated costs incurred in anticipation of fire, costs borne 'as a consequence' of fire and the cost of the Fire and Rescue Ser-vice. Average costs were also calculated for different types of fire. The DCLG tried to outsource the calculation of these data in 2011, but their proposed collection was neither feasible nor adequately funded even on a non-profit basis, and the statistics were discontinued in 2012.

By 2015, these developments meant that individual FRSs no longer had the tools and techniques, nor the databases and information, to make realistic comparisons at a national level about value for money, service performance or financial conformance. By that time DCLG had effectively taken away the national and local information and infrastructure that would allow them to do so. If they are assessed against the 4-stage performance management data model shown in Fig. 3.2, they would clearly be evaluated collectively as a data-poor environment.

Mrs May's response in 2016 was to propose a national database and central repository of information and to make it available on a publicly accessible website, although concerns around the comparability of such datasets would persist, given that individual FRSs have developed their own definitions and methodologies of data collection. As of November 2019, it has not as yet appeared.

In the absence of central support, co-ordination or guidance, therefore, individual fire and rescue services have continued to develop their data and information to facilitate their local emergency responses, but at the expense of consistency and comparability across the sector. Good practice, innovations and potential learning have not been routinely and systematically captured, nor consistently applied to improve services, other than in a few isolated cases. Operationally, fire and rescue services have apparently coped well, although the HMICFRS inspections suggest they could clearly have performed better. Strategically and nationally, and with the exception of the first two tranches of the inspections, the evidence base available to policy makers is as poor as it was in 2015.

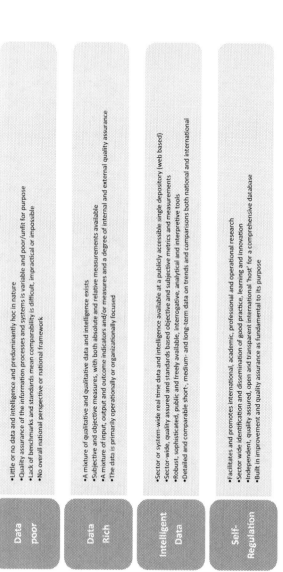

Data poor
- Little or no data and intelligence and predominantly hoc in nature
- Quality assurance of the information processes and systems is variable and poor/unfit for purpose
- Lack of benchmarks and standards mean comparability is difficult, impractical or impossible
- No overall national perspective or national framework

Data Rich
- A mixture of qualitative and qualitative data and intelligence exists
- Subjective and objective measures, with both absolute and relative measurements available
- A mixture of input, output and outcome indicators and/or measures and a degree of internal and external quality assurance
- The data is primarily operationally or organizationally focused

Intelligent Data
- Sector or system-wide real time data and intelligence available at a publicly accessible single depository (web based)
- Sector-wide, quality assured and standards based objective and subjective metrics and measurements
- Robust, sophisticated, public and freely available, interrogative, analytical and interpretive tools
- Detailed and comparable short-, medium- and long-term data on trends and comparisons both national and international

Self-Regulation
- Facilitates and promotes international, academic, professional and operational research
- Sector wide identification and dissemination of good practice, learning and innovation
- Independent, quality assured, open and transparent international 'host' for a comprehensive database
- Built in improvement and quality assurance as fundamental to its purpose

Fig. 3.2. The Performance Management 'Data Environment' Model.

3.3 CONTROL ROOMS

All fire and rescue services in England are responsible for accepting and processing emergency fire calls in their areas, and through agreements with neighbouring services during busy periods such as severe and widespread flooding. Dedicated control staff use computer-aided mobilising systems to locate the nearest resources and mobilise them to the incident. They are supported by caller identification location technology, satellite positioning equipment and mobile data terminals. They currently use the 'Airwave' radio system which originated as a public–private partnership with BT but is now owned by Motorola. There are similar control room arrangements in place for the police and ambulance services and all 107 police fire and ambulance services in England, Scotland and Wales use Airwave (see National Operational Guidance, 2019).

Emergency service control rooms have featured in many television programmes and are reasonably familiar to the general public. They are operated by relatively small teams but play a vital part of emergency response. The National Occupational Standard/Emergency fire services control operations guidance includes specific advice on control rooms, although these are not yet universally adopted.

The performance of these units is constantly scrutinised, internally and externally, and they are generally included in any fire investigations. The HMICFRS inspections published in 2018/19 found call handling to be broadly effective and the rooms to be operating under a range of operating models. Some rooms are specific to one fire and rescue service, and others are shared by several services: e.g. North West Control handles Lancashire, Greater Manchester, Cumbria and Cheshire together. The inspectors found that shared control rooms improved mobilisation across FRS borders.

In Kent and Merseyside there are co-located police and fire control rooms, although not yet an integrated police and fire control room. At the local and operational level, HMICFRS found that improvements in performance and cost-effectiveness have been gradual but continuous, partly due to some services adopting national protocols, guidance and standards. A number of control rooms were also diversifying into other roles e.g. taking 'careline' calls or giving post incident information on social media.

The two national and strategic projects that would potentially have directly affected control room performance, had they been implemented, are the 'FiReControl' project (NAO, 2011) and the proposed replacement of the 'Airwave' emergency communications system. The first was cancelled after 2010, whereas the second was still ongoing in Autumn 2019. Both are indicative of the strategic leadership, guidance and 'support' offered nationally to assist service delivery (NAO, 2011, 2019).

FiReControl commenced in 2004 and sought to reduce the number of fire control centres from 46 to 9 and use a national computer system to handle calls, mobilise equipment and manage incidents. It was cancelled in 2010, by which time it had spent £245m and the final completion estimate had increased to £635m – five times the original budget of £120m (NAO, 2011). This was a failure and an embarrassing public relations disaster for the government and the service. According to the NAO, FiReControl wasted a minimum of £469m and failed to provide any enhancement to the capacity of control centres over seven years (NAO, 2011). Further losses were made when the department failed in its attempt to persuade Fire and Rescue Services to use the empty regional control centres (DCLG, 2014). In this case it is worth quoting the comptroller general's introduction to his report in full.

*This is yet another example of a Government
IT project taking on a life of its own, absorbing ever-
increasing resources without reaching its objectives.
The rationale and benefits of a regional approach
were unclear and badly communicated to locally
accountable fire and rescue services who remained
unconvinced. Essential checks and balances in the
early stages of the project were ineffective. It was
approved on the basis of unrealistic estimates of costs
and under-appreciation of the complexity of the IT
involved and the project was hurriedly implemented
and poorly managed. Its legacy is the chain of
expensive regional control centres whose future is
uncertain.*

(Amyas Morse, Head of the National Audit Office)

The Emergency Services Network (ESN) is the government's chosen option to replace the Airwave system. It is intended to save money by sharing an existing commercial 4G network (unlike Airwave, which is fully dedicated to its users), and allow better use of mobile data. The technology therefore needs to give emergency services priority over other users of the network, in particular at times of urgent need or during crises. ESN would be used by the 107 emergency services in England, Scotland and Wales and by 363 other organisations in the public, private and third sectors. The project was commissioned by the Home Office in 2014 and ministers expected that the emergency services would start using ESN in September 2017, allowing Airwave to be replaced in December 2019. By 2017 the Home Office realised its plan for delivering ESN was not achievable. It commissioned an independent review and in September announced a 'reset' of its approach based on a phased introduction of ESN rather than cancellation and continued use of the costly Airwave

(Home Office, 2019; NAO, 2019). The airwave contract has, however, been extended to 'at least' 2020. In May 2019, the NAO found that there has been a 49% increase in forecast costs (now £9.3billion), £1.4 billion of which was attributable to the extension of the Airwave contract (NAO, 2019).

> *We reported on ESN in September 2016 and concluded that the Home Office was underrating the risks to delivering ESN successfully. By 2017, the Home Office realised that its plan for delivering ESN was not achievable……. The Home Office does not yet have a robust and sufficiently detailed plan that demonstrates that it understands the challenges faced by emergency services in introducing ESN, and it is also not clear how the various programme components of ESN will be integrated successfully…. There are still significant risks and, based on past performance, it seems unlikely that ESN can be delivered by the target date of 2022. If the Home Office is to bring this vital programme back on track and deliver the intended benefits, it must develop a comprehensive, integrated plan that addresses the significant uncertainties that remain.*
>
> (NAO, 2019, p. 1)

3.4 PREVENTION AND PROTECTIVE SERVICES

One of the most important but least surprising findings from both of the HMICFRS summary reports (2018a, 2019) is that protection and prevention services have been systematically under-resourced at the local level by Fire and Rescue Authorities and Services:

> *The consequences of long-term under-investment in this crucial area are too often evident. Protection*

> *teams often are not given a sufficiently large share of*
> *the service's resources to do their work. We saw this*
> *reflected in the 42 % reduction in the number of fire*
> *safety audits over the last seven years.*
>
> (HMICFRS, 2018a, p. 5)

> *We are still concerned about how services protect*
> *the public through the regulation of fire safety. ....*
> *All too often, protection teams are under-resourced*
> *to meet the expectations set in the service's risk-*
> *based inspection programme. In the absence of*
> *national standards and legislation, there is no*
> *consistent way in which services fulfil their*
> *protection responsibilities. Services vary*
> *considerably in how they define high-risk premises,*
> *the frequency of audits and the use of enforcement*
> *action. As a result, premises in one service area are*
> *often treated very differently from similar premises*
> *in another.*
>
> (HMICFRS, 2019, p. 5)

This merely confirms previous evidence at the local and national or aggregate level (see Murphy, Lakoma, et al. (2019) for a comparison of the contrasting priorities in England and Scotland). It is interesting that the Inspectorate's recommendation to address this is for action at the national level. The inspectors also found prevention and protection services, and individual projects, were 'very rarely' evaluated because FRSs did not have the tools, techniques, people skills or metrics to undertake this task. Techniques such as cost–benefit analysis and financial and social returns on expenditure are used extensively to do this in other public services, and Taylor, Appleton, Keen, and Fielding (2019) have recently shown how Merseyside FRS have created tools and techniques to measure the effectiveness of their fire prevention strategy. Using FRS, NHS and national statistics, Merseyside is assessing four areas:

- The overall effectiveness of FRS provision;
- Fire incidents, injuries and facilities compared to spend per head;
- The effectiveness of fire prevention strategies and
- The effectiveness of the targeting of fire prevention.

Despite such initiatives, prevention and protection services have been somewhat neglected since 2010, as FRSs try to cope with austerity cuts and a poor evidence base that makes it difficult to develop the case for investing in functions that are not on the 'front line' (Ferry & Murphy, 2015; Murphy, Ferry, et al., 2019; NAO, 2015). Yet, FRSs will struggle to meet their new statutory obligation to work collaboratively with other services if they cannot demonstrate they are measuring their returns on investment or achieving the benefits they anticipated.

3.5 CORPORATE AND MANAGEMENT SERVICES

The fundamental assurance that public money is being spent for the purpose it was intended and that value for money is being achieved in its expenditure is at the core of any definition of public interest. The quality and quantity of financial data available to fire and rescue services since 2010 were a central concern of the NAO (2015) and PAC (2016) reports.

The 2018/19 HMICFRS inspections found that 'all fire and rescue services would benefit from better access to accurate and robust financial data that is consistent across services' (2018a, 2018b, 2018c, p. 12). 'To manage budgets, use resources efficiently and effectively, and pursue opportunities to reduce costs, fire and rescue services need accurate and reliable data....and ... some services lack credible and comparable data about expenditure' (2019, p. 30).

This issue can only be tackled at the national level and HMICFRS began working with the Chartered Institute of Finance and Accountancy (CIPFA) to address these problems in 2018. However, the government and/or HMICFRS, together with CIPFA, also urgently need to address the main document where local financial information is brought together for the benefit of the public, namely the Statement of Assurance. This was introduced by the 2012 National Framework, but Spencer et al. (2019) found significant inconsistencies in its content and reporting: 30% of authorities did not have an up-to-date statement on their website, and there was confusion amongst authorities as to the statement's role. Together, these factors meant there was a significant risk that FRSs perceived it as a 'box ticking' exercise rather than a real contribution to public assurance.

One of the major inadequacies most consistently reported in the recent inspections by HMICFRS was in workforce and working practices, where inspectors simply asked how well the service looked after its people. Only 3 out of 14 in tranche 1, and 4 out of 16 in tranche 2 were ranked as good, and only Oxfordshire and Lancashire were ranked outstanding in any one of the 5 sub-categories (promoting the right values and culture in both cases) (HMICFRS, 2018a, 2019).

Inadequate data, information and basic systems are a key contributory factor in this situation. Fewer than half the services inspected had effective workforce planning systems, and poor information management systems meant that some services couldn't be sure whether their staff had had risk critical safety training. Some managers have no effective oversight of the hours their staff are working, or data about engine availability. The long-term deep-rooted issues of workforce diversity and its malevolent impact on organisational culture also persist in some services. Inspectors found that services inadequately prepared to deliver the pace and scale of workforce reform that is needed in the challenging circumstances that they face. Only 7 of the 30 services inspected in tranches 1 and 2 were graded as good for managing performance and developing leaders, and none was outstanding (HMICFRS, 2018a, 2019).

The use of information technology is another widespread corporate issue. The challenges of replacing the Airwave system have been discussed above, but HMICFRS found that at the local level 'too often staff are using antiquated, unreliable or at worst paper based systems to transfer vital information... and... on occasions firefighters are attending incidents without access to all the information that might help keep them and the public safe.'

(HMICFRS, 2018a, p. 15)

3.6 MULTI-AGENCY PARTNERSHIPS AND COLLABORATIONS

Fire and rescue services have been engaged in numerous statutory and non-statutory multi-agency partnerships and collaborations for many years. However, the Chapter 1 of the Policing and Crime Act 2017, together with the most recent National Framework, signalled a shift in emphasis, in that they stipulated that services should be delivered with a much greater emphasis on collaboration between the emergency services and other key stakeholders.

This impetus builds on the Joint Emergency Services Inter-operability Principles (JESIP) programme, which ran from 2012 to 2014 and aimed to improve the way the police, fire and rescue and ambulance services worked together when responding to major multi-agency incidents. JESIP's *Joint Doctrine: the interoperability framework* sets out a standard approach to multi-agency working, along with training and awareness tools to help organisations skill up their staff (JESIP, 2013). Whilst the initial focus was on improving the response to major incidents, its principles and models can be used in other environments where organisations need to work together more effectively. The current ambition is to encourage integrating the JESIP ways of working into all policies and procedures until staff use JESIP as a matter of course (JESIP, 2016).

Regarding collaboration, the evidence from the recent inspections at local levels suggests that:

> *Services are generally keen to explore collaboration opportunities and are willing to engage in initiatives with local organisations. For example, we have seen services sharing estates, creating joint control rooms and working on behalf of police and ambulance services. But not enough services are evaluating, reviewing and monitoring this work to understand whether they are achieving the benefits they anticipate.*
> (HMICFRS, 2019, p. 8)

As mentioned above, however, it is difficult to see how services are going to expand collaborations and joint working if they do not have the skills, data and systems to capture and measure the impact of their investments and demonstrate their benefits.

Fire and rescue services are universal services of a relatively consistent nature which regularly have to collaborate with other fire and rescue services, other emergency services and key partners such as local authorities. Since 2010, the former 'improvement' infrastructure provided collectively and collaboratively by the former Audit Commission, the Improvement & Development Agency, CIPFA, the Local Government Leadership Centre, the former Fire Inspectorate and the

Fire Service College has been significantly scaled back (Murphy, Ferry, et al., 2019). These organisations sought to continually improve the evidence base, question risk assessments and provide tools, techniques and systems for effective data management. They supported systemic and individual innovation and creativity, and pioneered and co-ordinated pathfinders, pilots, beacons, networks, benchmarking and sharing good practice.

Most of this work went into abeyance between 2010 and 2015, although recent inspection reports welcomed the more recent work that NFCC Central programme, JESIP, the LGA, CIPFA and others have either continued or committed to develop in these areas, albeit with reduced capacity and capabilities from the earlier arrangements.

3.7 CONCLUSIONS

This chapter has attempted to review the 'evidence base' for policy development, service delivery and assurance at local and national levels. The purpose was to try and identify which parts or areas of the collective evidence base for the performance management regime in fire and rescue services are inadequate or in some cases completely missing. In order to do this, we examined the different areas that data and information are needed and tried to identify which areas were well served by what is currently available and which areas are not so well served.

By looking at the five main functions of fire and rescue services individually, we can see that even the strongest area ('response services') have identifiable data and analytical capacity needs – at both national and local levels. Protection and prevention services, and to a lesser extent corporate and management services and support to develop collaborative initiatives, have much greater gaps and inadequacies.

Overall, we see from Fig. 3.2 that fire and rescue services at both national and local levels are currently having to contend with a 'data poor' operating environment. Historically the service has had a long attachment and strong adherence to evidence-based policy and service configuration (Ewen, 2010; Murphy & Greenhalgh, 2018). A service that has the public interest in the form of improving public safety as its key strategic intent, that bases its strategic and operational configuration on the basis of an assessment and management of risks, and is heavily dependent on collaborative planning and action is clearly appropriate to a Public Value perspective. This is in turn dependent on a robust and comprehensive evidence base. The dilemma is that the inadequacy of the evidence is acknowledged by government, inspectorate and the wider community of interest; the problem is that it will take a collective, collaborative co-productive approach to produce it.

REFERENCES

Department of Communities and Local Government. (2008). *Fire and rescue service national framework 2008–11.* London: TSO.

Department of Communities and Local Government. (2012). *Fire and rescue national framework for England.* London: TSO.

Ewen, S. (2010). *Fighting fires: Creating the British fire service, 1800–1978.* Basingstoke: Palgrave Macmillan.

Ferry, L., & Murphy, P. (2015). *Financial sustainability, accountability and transparency across local public service bodies in England under austerity.* Report to National Audit Office (NAO). Nottingham: NTU.

FIRE. (2018, June). UK ranked 34th in resilience to fire. *FIRE*, *113*(1409), 14.

Hackitt, J. (2018). *Building a safer future – Independent review of building regulations and fire safety: Final report*. London: Ministry of Housing, Communities and Local Government.

HM Inspectorate of Constabulary and Fire & Rescue Services. (2018a). *Fire and rescue service inspections 2018/19: Summary of findings from Tranche 1*. London: HMICFRS.

HM Inspectorate of Constabulary and Fire & Rescue Services. (2018b). Detailed judgement criteria. Retrieved from https://www.justiceinspectorates.gov.uk/hmicfrs/fire-and-rescue-services/how-we-inspect-fire-and-rescue-services/#judgments. Accessed on July 22, 2019.

HM Inspectorate of Constabulary and Fire & Rescue Services. (2018c). Public perceptions of fire and rescue services data 2017/18 (spreadsheets). Retrieved from https://www.justiceinspectorates.gov.uk/hmicfrs/fire-and-rescue-services/data/. Accessed on July 22, 2019.

HM Inspectorate of Constabulary and Fire & Rescue Services. (2019). *Fire and rescue service inspections 2018/19: Summary of findings from Tranche 2*. London: HMICFRS.

Home Office. (2019). Emergency Services Network: Overview (updated 26 June 2019). Retrieved from https://www.gov.uk/government/publications/the-emergency-services-mobile-communications-programme/emergency-services-network. Accessed on December 16, 2019.

Joint Emergency Services Interoperability Programme. (2013). Joint Doctrine: The interoperability Programme. Retrieved from https://www.jesip.org.uk/what-is-the-joint-doctrine. Accessed on December 16, 2019.

Joint Emergency Services Interoperability Programme. (2016). Joint Doctrine: Edition two. Retrieved from https://www.jesip.org.uk/what-is-the-joint-doctrine. Accessed on December 16, 2019.

Lewis, B. (2017). Fire Minister's speech to reform. Retrieved from https://www.gov.uk/government/speeches/fire-ministers-speech-to-reform. Accessed on July 26, 2019.

May, T. (2016). *Home Secretary speech on fire reform.* London: Home Office.

Murphy, P., & Ferry, L. (2018). Another turn of the screw: Fire and rescue under the coalition government of 2010–2015 (Chapter 4). In P. Murphy & K. Greenhalgh (Eds.), *Fire and rescue services leadership and management perspectives* (pp. 45–60). London: Springer.

Murphy, P., Ferry, L., Glennon, R., & Greenhalgh, K. (2019a). *Public service accountability: Rekindling a debate.* Cham: Palgrave Macmillan.

Murphy, P., & Glennon, R. (2018, March). Why not take the time to get the fire framework right? *FIRE, 113,* 21–23.

Murphy, P., & Greenhalgh, K. (2018). *Fire and rescue services: Leadership and management perspectives. Leadership and management in emergency services.* London: Springer.

Murphy, P., Greenhalgh, K., & Parkin, C. (2012). Fire and rescue service reconfiguration: A case study in Nottinghamshire. *International Journal of Emergency Services, 1*(1), 86–94.

Murphy, P., Lakoma, K., & Toothill, A. (2019b, June). Do we need to review IRMPs? *FIRE, 114,* 13–16.

National Audit Office. (2011). *Department for Communities and Local Government: The failure of the FiReControl project.* London: NAO.

National Audit Office. (2015). *Department for Communities and Local Government: Financial sustainability of fire and rescue services*. London: NAO.

National Audit Office. (2019). *Progress delivering the emergency services network*. London: NAO.

National Fire Chief's Council. (2018a, July). Professional standards – Briefing note. Retrieved from https://www. nationalfirechiefs.org.uk/write/MediaUploads/committee %20documents/Standards%20Board/PSB_Project_-_Briefing_ Note__July_2018.pdf. Accessed on July 22, 2019.

National Fire Chief's Council. (2018b). Professional standards board project business case. Retrieved from http://lga. moderngov.co.uk/documents/s16731/PSB%20Board%20 Paper%201%20-%20Professional%20Standards%20 Business%20Case.pdf. Accessed on July 22, 2019.

National Operational Guidance. (2019). Emergency fire control room guidance. Retrieved from https://www.ukfrs.com/ guidance/operations. Accessed on December 16, 2019.

Public Accounts Committee. (2016). *Financial sustainability of fire and rescue services*. Twenty-third report of session 2015–16. London: TSO.

Spencer, T., Hayden, J., Murphy, P., & Glennon, R. (2019). Stating the obvious: Evaluating the state of public assurance in fire and rescue authorities in England. *International Journal of Emergency Services*, 8(1), 20–33.

Taylor, M., Appleton, D., Keen, G., & Fielding, J. (2019). Assessing the effectiveness of fire prevention strategies. *Public Money & Management*, 39(6), 418–427.

4

TWO STEPS FORWARD AND ONE BACK: THE 2018 NATIONAL FRAMEWORK

4.1 INTRODUCTION

This chapter investigates the history, antecedents and drivers for the new Fire and Rescue National Framework for England that was published on the 8 May 2018 (Home Office, 2018). A performance regime or a national framework is a set of priorities, objectives, requirements and ideals that frame an entire service and give it direction. It can be defined as 'the context, the parameters, the agencies and the relationships operating within the three domains of policy development, service delivery and public assurance in public services' (Murphy, Lakoma, & Glennon, 2018).

The 2018 version of the framework replaced the 2012 version and is the fifth national framework to be published for English Fire and Rescue Services since the 2004 Fire and Rescue Services Act introduced national frameworks to the sector. The government has a duty under the Act to produce the framework and keep it current, and the act also requires the Home Secretary to report every two years on fire and rescue authorities' compliance with the framework. Fire and Rescue Authorities represent the political level of Fire and Rescue's governance, and fire and rescue services as well as authorities must have regard to the framework in carrying out their duties.

The purpose of this chapter is to review previous national frameworks for the Fire and Rescue Services in order to critically evaluate the 2018 framework in its contemporary English context. These types of framework typically embrace some or all of the three interrelated domains of policy formulation and development; the management and monitoring of service delivery; and the assurance that is provided to key stakeholders – most notably the government, the service itself, its key collaborators, and the public (Murphy, Wankhade, & Lakoma, 2019).

Each of the three domains has a number of constituent elements, some of which will overlap or operate in more than one domain and some of which will operate or be specific to a particular domain. Thus in the case of Fire and Rescue, Fig. 2.1 below illustrates the generic elements that have

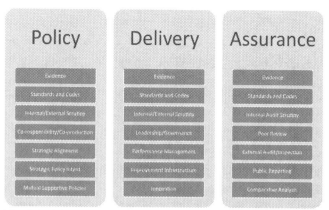

Fig. 2.1. The Three Domains of Policy Formulation, Service Delivery and Public Assurance.

appeared in the three domains within the successive national frameworks for fire and rescue services since they were introduced in 2004, although not all elements have been specifically addressed in every iteration of the framework. Identifying the constituent elements is, however, helpful for exploring the efficacy of the various frameworks.

These domains are not however unfettered. As explained in Chapter 2 they are in practice situated within national (and sometimes international or supranational) parameters which constrain the operational activity of the three domains. These parameters are not static in the long term as they may be subject to political change and strategic public service reforms, but they do tend to provide context and some stability, at least in the short term. The three most common parameters that are identified in the illustrative model in Chapter 2 are the prevailing legislative provision (both national and international); the short, medium and/or long term resources available to the service or sector; and the strategic and operational landscapes of organisations and institutions currently extant within the service or sector (see Fig. 2.1 in Chapter 2). These three very tangible parameters are shown as informing, constraining and/or regulating the policy/delivery/assurance domains and interacting on each other in Fig. 2.1.

The final contextual parameters are more intangible, but no less real and important. The three domains of policy development, service delivery and public assurance, as well as the broader national and international parameters, are themselves both informed by, and subject to, a prevailing set of values or norms (either implicit or explicit), which define the behaviours, organisational culture and standards that are considered appropriate in public services in every part of the regime. Within the UK these values and norms are currently known as the Nolan principles (see Chapter 2).

4.2 BACKGROUND AND CONTEXT

The Fire and Rescue Service in England has experienced considerable reform over the last 20 years. Service modernisation and the introduction of new public management theory characterised public service policy in the first few years of the New Labour administrations. This was followed by a greater emphasis on prevention and protection, as well as changes in external assurance mechanisms and organisations in the latter half of the Labour administrations, which also saw the abolition of the former Her Majesty's Fire Service Inspectorate. From 2010 onwards, a retreat from service improvement as the principal concern of public service reform (Glennon, 2017); the rise of austerity localism (Lowndes & Pratchett, 2012) and public expenditure cutbacks dominated policy under the Coalition administration, as well as more specific pressure for greater integration of blue light services (Murphy & Greenhalgh, 2018a).

Following critical reports from the NAO (2015) and the Public Accounts Committee (2016), the government acknowledged the need for radical change (Home Office, 2017a) and enshrined facilitating amendments in the Policing and Crime Bill, which later emerged as Chapters 1–4 of the Policing and Crime Act 2017. These included express intentions to improve the evidence base available for developing policy and delivering services, to change governance arrangements through the introduction of Police Fire and Crime Commissioners, and to establish institutions such as a new Professional Standards Body, a new inspectorate and inspection regime and a new National Fire Chiefs Council (May, 2016). All of these are intended to inform or lead to better policy development, improve services delivery and provide greater public assurance. They also rendered the 2012 National Framework unfit for purpose if not functionally obsolete.

Chapter 3 covered the changes in the evidence base and the systems, processes, tools and mechanisms for analysing, interpreting or interrogating the available information. The following sections will critically evaluate the five national fire and rescue frameworks published to date culminating in the 2018 framework, using the model as a general guide to illustrate their strengths, or weaknesses and any omissions. The re-establishment of an external inspection regime and a new inspectorate will be discussed in Chapter 5.

4.2.1 The 2004–2006 National Frameworks

The first National Framework for Fire and Rescue Service (2004–2006) was introduced by the second New Labour administration under Tony Blair. The framework also included an implementation plan for the radical new arrangements to be introduced by the 2004 Act, which sought to 'modernise' the service in terms of its governance, performance management service delivery and accountability arrangements (Murphy & Greenhalgh, 2018b). It was introduced in parallel with the new Fire and Rescue Services Act and the Civil Contingencies Act of 2004. The former gave statutory backing to the framework.

Devolution of powers to Scotland and Wales meant the framework only applied to England. It embraced continuous improvement as the primary strategic intent, aligned to co-production and collective responsibility in policy and service delivery, and the achievement of value for money based on economy, efficiency and effectiveness. The framework stipulated that the government and fire authorities must work in partnership to address wicked issues and achieve shared goals: 'Only by working together can central and local government achieve these targets' (ODPM, 2004, p. 4). The framework stressed the importance of public service improvement and introduced performance management and greater public assurance across the sector, supported by copious new data, operational and technical guidance including the rollout of the Fire Service Emergency Cover (FSEC) Toolkit. It linked the sector's objectives to national Public Service Agreements and the Spending Review. It introduced a greater focus on prevention, protection and collaborative working across public services, than had previously been the case (Murphy & Greenhalgh, 2018b). It strengthened external audit and assurance arrangements, introducing the possibility of government intervention in underperforming services.

The framework committed government, fire authorities and services to achieving long-term reductions in fire deaths and deliberate fires and introduced both the concept and a formal requirement to produce Integrated Risk Management Plans (IRMPs), assisted by a new toolkit of data, tools and guidance (ODPM, 2006a). These plans were to be based on a new assessment of the pattern of fire risk to individuals and communities. Prior to 2004, the configuration of fire service resources (premises, appliances, equipment, work patterns etc.), was essentially based on historical developments and the response times to fire incidents and vulnerable premises and buildings (Murphy & Greenhalgh, 2014a, 2018b).

> *The old, national standards of fire cover, which set out the speed and weight of response to fire depending on building density, were insufficiently flexible to allow Fire and Rescue Authorities to respond to the needs of their communities. They focused exclusively on risk to property rather than risk to life, and did not take account of the serious non-fire incidents to which the Service responds.*
> (ODPM, 2004, p. 8).

This first framework dealt with nearly all of the issues in our generic model, although it did not deal in any detail with financial support. It contained substantial changes to fire and rescue policy, service delivery and public assurance arrangement. The area where the framework was most controversial was the introduction of a 'regional approach' and, in particular, the creation of Regional Management Boards to deal with six key areas of work. They aimed to:

- put in place effective resilience plans for large scale emergencies;

- introduce regional personnel and human resource functions;

- develop a regional approach to training;

- establish regional control centres; and

- introduce regional procurement within the context of a national procurement strategy.

The unfortunate history of regional control centres has already been examined in Chapter 3. Although some of the remaining regional initiatives lasted longer than others, not one has stood the test of time, with the exception of the new arrangements for dealing with large scale emergencies – which have to cross boundaries whether local regional or national (Murphy & Greenhalgh, 2014b).

In addition, the government sought to introduce the framework at a time when the sector was pre-occupied with the introduction of the new Integrated Performance Development System. This had resulted from the resolution of the second national strike over pay and conditions (Andrews & Ashworth, 2018). Although relations between the government and the sector were improving, they were still fragile, and this made implementation more difficult.

4.2.2 The 2006–2008 Framework

The second national framework (ODPM, 2006b), which quickly followed, similarly covered a three-year period and not surprisingly on the surface it bears a striking resemblance to the first. Its scope and ambition were similar, in that it sought to provide a comprehensive framework, but it introduced new and more ambitious objectives and took a longer-term perspective by aiming to integrate rather than just align the service with wider public reforms of locally delivered services. The first framework attempted to modernise the fire and rescue organisations and the first fire assessments were essentially *service* evaluations. In contrast, the second included organisational assessments that intended to encourage co-operation and bring the sector and its locally based organisations into alignment with other local public services in their communities and the overall public service improvement agenda. The second framework therefore attempted to provide a comprehensive policy and operating framework for the service to complement, and work in parallel with, the contemporary performance management and assurance regime for the local government sector developed by the Audit Commission, as well as the parallel performance regimes that were developing in the health and police services.

The second framework therefore complemented and embraced Comprehensive Performance Assessments and Local Public Service Agreements. Comprehensive Performance Assessments were the new organisational-wide assessments of local authorities introduced in 2005/2006, Local Public Service Agreements were agreements between central government and local authorities whereby local public service delivery organisations were rewarded for improved performance against mutually agreed targets in priority policy areas. The framework attempted to introduce a 'consistent vision to support strategic planning' (ODPM, 2006b, p. 3), and there was a new additional emphasis on the delivery of equality and diversity within the service (Andrews & Ashworth, 2018; Clarke, 2018). It also introduced the 'Use of Resources' assessment used in both the Local Government and healthcare assessment regimes (Audit Commission, 2009a; Campbell-Smith, 2008).

As with the first framework, it included a series of annexes which attempted to interpret and apply the responsibilities and relationships of all organisations in what, by now, was a rapidly changing organisational landscape at both strategic and operational levels. If the first framework had determined that greater collaboration would happen, the second helped answer how it would happen and who would be responsible specifically in relation to fire and rescue services. For example, although annex A reiterated the application of the protocol on central government engagement with poorly performing authorities (ODPM, 2006b, p. 70), this was interpreted through bespoke guidance for fire and rescue authorities issued to the Fire and Rescue Improvement Support Team (Coleman, 2009). Annex B laid out the new national FRS targets and the government's strategic priorities, while annex C reiterated the memorandum of understanding between Government and the Audit Commission concerning FRS in England. Annex D had new performance indicators and F listed operational and technical guidance.

Although the Fire and Rescue sector was initially resistant and relatively late to engage with the improvement agenda, it benefited from the government, the regulators and its key strategic partners' learning from engagement with other sectors (Murphy & Greenhalgh, 2018c). Indeed, 2005–2008 saw significant improvement in the co-production and delivery of policy, service delivery and public assurance (Audit Commission, 2005, 2006, 2007, 2008b, 2009b; Murphy et al., 2019;

Murphy & Greenhalgh, 2018c). The one area that remained contentious was the regional agenda and the regional management boards. Proposed in the first framework and established by the second, these boards struggled to gain the anticipated ownership, engagement and support across the sector that was assumed in the second framework and was critical to its success.

The second framework sought alignment of local objectives and priorities and complemented a longer-term national vision that the sector could generally buy into (ODPM, 2006b). The evidence base, although not yet strong, was improving and was assisted by considerable external support from a maturing improvement infrastructure that included the local government improvement agency, the leadership school and peer support as well as support from the Audit Commission and the government.

4.2.3 The 2008–2011 Framework

The third framework from 2008 to 2011 (DCLG, 2008) was intended to contribute to, complement and embrace the 'one-place' agenda of Gordon Brown's administration and the Comprehensive Area Assessments and Local Area Agreements that characterised local service policy and delivery from 2007 to 2010 (Murphy & Greenhalgh, 2018c). Following the Local Government Act and the Comprehensive Spending Review of 2007, the one-place initiative reflected a much greater focus on local rather than national priorities. It brought together performance information about the key locally delivered public services in every community across England. These were the services provided by local authorities, primary care trusts, the local criminal justice system and fire and rescue services. The views and assessments of six independent inspectorates: namely the Audit Commission, the Care Quality Commission, Ofsted, and Her Majesty's Inspectorates of Constabulary, Prisons and Probation were integrated into one system of assessment and reporting. It provided a combination of reports on individual organisational performance and a combined 'area' or aggregated score. All fire and rescue services therefore received both an 'Organisational Assessment' and an 'Area Assessment'. The former combined the Audit Commission's judgements on Managing Performance and 'Use of Resources' which were essentially operational and financial appraisals, respectively. The latter was based around the performance in delivering the Local Area Agreement and was carried out by the Joint Inspectorates and co-ordinated by the Audit Commission (Audit Commission, 2008a; Murphy & Greenhalgh, 2018c).

The framework itself was much slimmed down from its predecessors, it covered three years, and had only four chapters, reflecting the mutual confidence and involvement in its co-production between government and the sector. It again signalled another change in strategic intent or emphasis. The onset of the recession saw early references to the tighter fiscal climate, while the widespread flooding of 2007 had brought local, regional and national resilience into prominence. The one-place vision of the 2007 Local Government Act and the 2006 Strong and Prosperous Communities white paper had encouraged and facilitated greater cooperation and collaboration across public services, and the application of the government's recent equality and diversity strategy to the service commandeered the whole of one of its four chapters. As with its two predecessors, it was based on the IRMP and gave prevention and protection as much prominence as response. The roles of Regional Management Boards were now reduced to facilitating collaboration and working with Regional Control Centres. Apart from facilitating regional resilience boards and responses to emergencies, which had gained early acceptance, there was no mention of a 'regional agenda'. However, this framework did propose significant improvements and developments to the evidence base and the government's research programme, together with a new Fire Research Academy. Authorities were also instructed to be ready to implement the new electronic Incident Recording System by April 2009.

Both the academic literature and inspection reports suggest that between 2005 and 2010, the performance of fire and rescue services was consistently improving across the sector, in terms of organisational and financial management, and collaboration (Audit Commission, 2008b, 2009b; Coleman, 2009; Murphy & Greenhalgh, 2018c; Murphy, Greenhalgh, Ferry, & Glennon, 2019). However, as the third framework was being prepared for publication in May 2008, the economic and political outlooks were significantly changing at both national and local political levels, and this influenced its content and implementation.

Despite the fire sector demonstrating considerable potential for further improvement and being one of the fastest improving sectors (Murphy & Greenhalgh, 2018c; Murphy et al., 2019), the all-party political consensus around public service reform and the performance management arrangements was starting to disintegrate. The 2007 general election was much closer in terms of the popular vote than had been anticipated and after a decade of New Labour national governments the control of local councils and the Local Government Association was overwhelmingly Conservative. As mentioned above, by late 2007 the challenges of the impending recession were becoming evident. Traditional adversarial two-party politics were re-emerging, and the Conservative opposition was withdrawing from the consensus around public service reform and improvement based on investment in local services (Audit Commission, 2009c). When the CAA results emerged in 2009 it revealed a correlation between area affluence and the top scores (Bowcott, 2009). The Conservative Party then announced that it would abolish the CAA if it formed a government.

> *Labour have created an army of clipboard inspectors to monitor councils, which has done nothing to stop council tax doubling or frontline services like weekly bin collections being cut. Conservatives will abolish the bureaucratic CAA, and target inspection where it's really needed.* (Caroline Spelman, Shadow Secretary for Communities and Local Government (cited in Bowcott, 2009)).

When compared to the generic model it is clear the framework still had almost all of the key elements although many were still in early stages of development. However, while the third framework was probably the most comprehensive and coherent of all the national frameworks for fire and rescue services, its interdependence with the CAA, the continued increase in investment and the prominence and priority it afforded to workforce diversity and equality made it vulnerable to changes in political control in Westminster and at the Local Government Association.

4.2.4 The 2012 Framework

The strategic intent of government towards all public services changed in 2010. Prior to 2010 the strategic intent and dominant policy objective was continuous improvement in policy development, service delivery and assurance to the public. After 2010 the dominant macro-economic policy objective became the attempt to reduce the structural deficit on the national debt, primarily through significant reductions in public expenditure. The Conservative-Lib Dem Coalition's programme for government in 2010 stated:

> *The deficit reduction programme takes precedence over any of the other measures in this agreement, and the speed of implementation of any measures that have a cost to the public finances will depend on decisions to be made in the Comprehensive Spending Review.*
> (HMG, 2010, p. 35).

The short-term policy of cutback management initiated by Osborne in 2010, and continued by his successor Philip Hammond, had by 2019 endured for nine years and over 17 budget or financial statements. It has dominated fiscal policy at both national and local levels during this period. If cutback management is ever efficient or effective in reducing the distribution of public resources, it is as an immediate or short-term response to a crisis or financial shock. In the medium to long term, a more strategic response is required to ensure economy, efficiency and effectiveness of public expenditure (Packard, Patti, Daly, Tucker-Tatlow, & Farrell, 2007; Schmidt, Groeneveld, & Van de Walle, 2017). This fiscal-centric macroeconomic policy also led to a narrowing of the scope and focus within individual public policies, policy-making and policy development. This was later made explicit in the 2018 framework but was left implicit in 2012. Nevertheless, it served to restrict the potential for service improvement from performance management regimes in the post-2010 period.

The period of the Coalition Government, between May 2010 and May 2015, was dominated by long-term public sector expenditure reductions, 'austerity localism' (Featherstone, Ince, Mackinnon, Straus, & Cumbers, 2012; Lowndes & Pratchett, 2012) and considerable uncertainty within public services in England, as short-term cutback management endured long beyond its original timescale (Blyth, 2013; O'Hara, 2015). Although the government initially questioned whether a national framework was necessary (DCLG, 2010), the fourth national framework was published in 2012. It was as short, if not shorter, than its immediate predecessors, and addressed a range of new challenges and risks, including the threat of terrorism, an ageing population and the impact of climate change, and had to balance these against the need to significantly reduce spending (DCLG, 2012).

It was the first policy or framework to be addressed exclusively to Fire and Rescue Authorities rather than to the fire service and the fire 'community'. It reflected the wider shift in policy development from co-production and collaborative working across the sector towards a greater emphasis on local accountability between the public services and residents (Murphy & Ferry, 2018). The public service improvement infrastructure that facilitated service improvement and multi-agency collaborations was almost totally dismantled in the misnamed 'bonfire of the quangos' (Institute for Government, 2012) and with it much of the pre-existing evidence base on which policy and delivery depended (Dommett & Flinders, 2015; Hood, 1980). Following David Cameron's' localism agenda and his Open Government white papers (Cabinet Office, 2011, 2012), it moved accountability for the service from central government and placed responsibilities into the hands of local communities, as represented by fire authorities. It gave authorities more flexibility and freedom to deliver services but at the same time, his chancellor George Osborne was reducing central government financial support which was restricting their ability to act flexibly. In a move that exacerbated this situation in many areas, in 2012, the government abandoned the assessment of local needs based on multiple deprivation indices as the basis of the annual financial settlements for local services, which meant the pattern of spending on public services became less and less related to individual and community needs (Gray & Barford, 2018; Travers, Amin-Smith, Murphy, & Whiteman, 2019). The Local Audit and Accountability Act 2014 introduced a narrower focus on financial resources and short-term financial reporting rather than the broader 'Use of Resources' and the medium and long-term planning that was part of its predecessor.

This combination resulted in a vacuum in leadership, a deterioration in performance and rising risks to public safety and to the service achieving value for money, which was all laid bare in the NAO and Public Accounts Select Committee reports of 2015 and 2016. As quoted earlier, Theresa May in her last speech as Home Secretary was forced to acknowledge

> It is currently almost impossible to scrutinise your local fire and rescue service. There's no independent inspectorate; no regular audit of performance; and only limited available data on performance over time or between areas.
>
> (Theresa May MP. Home Office, 2016, p. 8).

The NAO report identified the Department of Communities and Local Government as the primary culprit, as it had effectively abdicated responsibility, withdrawn support and made it impossible for services to meet their national and local obligations and objectives. National policy was ineffectual, service delivery had significantly deteriorated and there were real and rising risks to the services achieving value for money (Murphy et al., 2019; NAO, 2015; PAC, 2016). The loss of national and local databases and information meant policy-making and service delivery at national and local levels (including the evidence base for IRMPs) became increasingly ad hoc and uncoordinated (Murphy et al., 2019). Responsibility for the service was transferred back to the Home Office in January 2016 after the NAO report had been published.

By 2016, the 2012 national framework had effectively become obsolete and Theresa May promised extensive changes to the governance, accountability and delivery of fire and rescue services via the Policing and Crime Act 2017. Before all this could be translated into a new framework however, there were further significant changes in the government's core policy objectives about to emerge from the General Election and European Referendum of 2016. 'Brexit' became (and remains at the time of writing) the dominant policy agenda of the subsequent national governments of both Theresa May and Boris Johnson.

4.2.5 The 2018 Framework

The new framework (Home Office, 2018) needed to reflect and operationalise the fire-related provisions in the Policing and Crime Act 2017, which included transforming local governance by encouraging Police and Crime Commissioners to take on responsibility for FRS provided a local case can be made. It contained a commitment to incorporate the recommendations of the Grenfell Tower inquiry and Dame Judith Hackitt's independent review of the Building Regulations (Hackitt, 2018) whenever these became available. The 2017 spending review had reconfirmed the constantly diminishing resource envelope up until 2022 and continuation of the policy of cutback management for public services.

The 2018 Framework itself reiterated that three key pillars and/or objectives of the service remained. FRSs had to identify, analyse and articulate risks in IRMPs; give greater priority to prevention and protection services, and provide greater accountability to local communities and the public. The 2018 framework included two 'additional' objectives, which had been prominent in earlier frameworks but were absent from the 2012 version. Improved collaboration between the three blue light emergency services was required by Chapter 1 of the 2017 Act, and the development of a resilient, skilled, flexible and diverse workforce was reintroduced into national policy having been omitted in 2012.

As detailed in Chapter 3, the data and intelligence upon which policy, service delivery and public assurance was to be based needed to be significantly improved, although this (and the dedicated website to host such information) has yet to materialise. The government helped to strengthen the service's internal collective leadership as the Association of Chief Fire Officers was encouraged to evolve into the National Fire Chief's Council (NFCC) with additional responsibilities for the reform agenda. It also announced that a new Fire Standards Board would be created to ensure professional standards are co-ordinated nationally. This would be independent of government and supported by the NFCC, which would produce the new standards. However, there would be no additional resources from government to assist any of these initiatives.

In terms of policy, and unlike the pre-2010 period, there has been an almost complete absence of piloting, pathfinding, option appraisal or scenario testing in policy-making. Formal public consultations, if undertaken at all, have largely ignored the Sedley/Gunning principles (Consultation Institute, 2018) for public consultations, have minimised the consultation periods and focused on specific questions that policy makers deem appropriate for a response (HMICFRS, 2017, 2018; Home Office, 2017b; Murphy & Greenhalgh, 2015; Murphy & Glennon, 2018). Some government consultations, such as those on intervention protocols and statements of assurance, have been published and multiple responses received but have not resulted in any changes or even any explanation as to why the government chose to ignore them (Murphy, Lakoma & Glennon, 2018; Spencer, Hayden, Murphy, & Glennon, 2019). In addition to the waste of public money, this suggests policy has been uninformed by wider national and international perspectives and that policy makers have been reluctant to learn from acknowledged good practice, from previous frameworks or from frameworks in alternative services or sector (Murphy, 2019).

The two major initiatives introduced by the 2017 Act and the national framework intended to improve service performance and increase public assurance were the introduction of Police, Fire and Crime Commissioners (PFCC) to the increasingly complicated governance landscape of fire and rescue services (Murphy et al., 2019), and the establishment of an independent inspection regime, under the reconstituted Her Majesty's Inspectorate of Constabulary and Fire & Rescue Services (HMICFRS). The new inspectorate and its inspection regime will be dealt with in more detail in the next chapter, but it is interesting to note at this stage, that the first round of inspections for all fire and rescue services did not include any assessment of their governance arrangements as the bodies that determine and prioritise their policy and resources which would have included PFCC's.

To date only four services (Essex, Northamptonshire, Staffordshire and North Yorkshire) have adopted the PFCC model, another (Cambridgeshire) has Home Office approval while the proposal in West Mercia (which involves both Hereford and Worcester FRS and Shropshire FRS) has overcome a judicial review to its plans. Two of these services (Essex and Northamptonshire) had significant long term, financial and performance issues resulting in external interventions that resulted in serious loss of public support and government confidence in the previous authorities (Caller, 2018; Lucas, 2015). All six are in Conservative-controlled local authority areas where the PFCC has also been Conservative. They have involved either county authorities (Northamptonshire), or combined fire authorities (Cambridgeshire, Essex, North Yorkshire, Stafford-shire, Hereford & Worcester and Shropshire). There are none in metropolitan authority areas or in London (which is exempt from these legislative provisions). To date all have proposed the same governance model with none of the PFCCs seeking to be a 'single employer' of staff. Four of the services involved (Cam-bridgeshire, Northants, Herford & Worcester and Shropshire) had had their first inspection by HMICFRS at the time of writing, while three (Essex, Staffordshire and North Yorkshire) were scheduled to be in the final (3rd) tranche, and therefore it is clearly too early to evaluate the impact on performance.

When evaluating the 2018 framework against the model, initial indications about the 2018 framework appear to show that the government is pulling back from the position announced by Theresa May and her ministers in 2016 and 2017. The duty to collaborate has been limited to the three emergency services and does not apply to wider partners such as local authorities, housing providers or welfare agencies, which are significant contributors to the success of long-term prevention and protection ambitions. Attempts to align the strategic and operational organisational landscape and the policy-delivery-assurance regime have been only partially successful, with some alignment around gover-nance (PFCC) and some operational emergency service integration, but this largely relates to response and back office services.

The remit and scope of the HMICFRS and its inspections is considered in the next chapter, but it is more limited than first anticipated and the 'robust and independent' inspectorate appears to have a much more nuanced relationship with the Home Office than its predecessor did with the Communities and Local Government department. Indeed, Home Office engagement and leadership appears unenthusiastic at best, and resembles the policy of benign neglect inherited by the Fire Minister Nick Raynsford when responsibility for the fire service was transferred from the Home Office to the Department of Transport Local Government and Regions in May 2001 (Raynsford, 2016). The improvements to the evidence base and the establishment of new standards and codes are (at best) taking longer to materialise than promised, and the government's first proposals responding to the Hackitt Report suggest that it will water down her recommended changes to the Building Regulations (LABV, 2019; MHCLG, 2019). Overall, therefore, the evidence to date suggests that political expediency and speed of delivery have had greater priority than facilitating improving services, increasing public safety and providing assurance to the public. As such, the 2018 framework represents a case of two steps forward being followed by one step back in almost all of its key components.

Ideally, the safety of the public, with a clear commitment to comprehensive improvement of the strategic and operational regime for the service, should be at the core of any fire and rescue national framework (as its unequivocal 'strategic intent'). It should also, in our opinion, re-establish the primacy of evidence-based policy and decision-making and have concrete proposals for improving data, information systems, accessibility and interrogation. Fire services are organised and configured as a response to the nature and level of risks to people, buildings and premises, and it is clear that the risk assessment and the current IRMPs need comprehensive review and central co-ordination to ensure consistency across the country (Murphy et al., 2019). In addition, the regime should replace the short-term financial appraisal with a 'use of resources' type assessment that is capable of supporting and evaluating short, medium and long-term resource strategies. It would also reverse the disproportionate decrease in invest-ment in protection and preventative strategies and clarify the scope and boundary issues between professional and technical or performance standards, while simultaneously providing a comprehensive and robust range of both. The latest version of England's framework does not address either of these issues in a satisfactory manner.

REFERENCES

Andrews, R., & Ashworth, R. (2018). Feeling the heat? Management reform and workforce diversity in the English fire service. In P. Murphy & K. Greenhalgh (Eds.), *Fire and rescue services: Leadership and management perspectives* (pp. 145–158). Cham: Springer.

Audit Commission. (2005). *Comprehensive performance assessment: Learning from CPA for the fire and rescue service in England 2005*. London: Audit Commission.

Audit Commission. (2006). *Fire and rescue – Performance framework 2006/07*. London: Audit Commission.

Audit Commission. (2007). *Fire and rescue comprehensive performance assessment 2007–2009*. London: Audit Commission.

Audit Commission. (2008a). *Comprehensive area assessment framework document*. London: Audit National Report.

Audit Commission. (2008b). *Fire and rescue performance assessment, scores and analysis of performance in fire and rescue authorities 2007*. London: Audit Commission.

Audit Commission. (2009a). *Final score – The impact of the comprehensive performance assessment of local government 2002–08*. London: Audit Commission.

Audit Commission. (2009b). *Fire and rescue performance assessment, 2009 – Scores and analysis of fire and rescue authorities performance 2008*. London: Audit Commission Community Safety National Report.

Audit Commission. (2009c). *Comprehensive area assessment: Perceptions audit and influence map*. London: Audit Commission.

Blyth, M. (2013). *Austerity: The history of a dangerous idea*. New York, NY: Oxford University Press.

Bowcott, O. (2009). Councils named and shamed by online audit of public services from bins to jails. *The Guardian*. p.1. Retrieved from https://www.theguardian.com/society/2009/dec/09/oneplace-website-council-services. Accessed on September 11, 2019.

Cabinet Office. (2011). *Open public services white paper*. London: Cabinet Office.

Cabinet Office. (2012). *Open public services*. London: Cabinet Office.

Caller, M. (2018). *Northamptonshire county council best value inspection*. Northampton: Northampton County Council.

Campbell-Smith, D. (2008). *Follow the money: The Audit Commission, public money and the management of public services 1983–2008*. London: Allen Lane.

Clarke, J. (2018). The use of equality and equality frameworks by Fire and Rescue Services. In P. Murphy & K. Greenhalgh (Eds.), *Fire and rescue services: Leadership and management perspectives* (pp. 159–179). Cham: Springer.

Coleman, P. (2009). *Fire and rescue improvement: A report prepared for DCLG on the approach and lessons learned*

2005–2009. Fire and Rescue Improvement Support Team DCLG. Unpublished.

Consultation Institute. (2018). *The Gunning principles – Implications.* Retrieved from https://www.consultation institute.org/the-gunning-principles-implications/. Accessed on August 20, 2019.

Department of Communities and Local Government. (2008). *Fire and rescue service national framework 2008–11.* London: Department for Communities and Local Government. London: The Stationery Office. Retrieved from https://assets.publishing.service.gov.uk/government/ uploads/system/uploads/attachment_data/file/7535/national framework200811.pdf. Accessed on July 26, 2019.

Department of Communities and Local Government. (2010). *Leading a lean and efficient fire and rescue service.* Retrieved from https://www.gov.uk/government/speeches/ leading-a-lean-and-efficient-fire-and-rescue-service. Accessed on August 20, 2019.

Department of Communities and Local Government. (2012). *Fire and rescue national framework for England.* London: The Stationery Office.

Dommett, K., & Flinders, M. (2015). The politics of quangocide. *Policy & Politics, 43,* (1), 3–25(23).

Featherstone, D., Ince, A., Mackinnon, D., Straus, K., & Cumbers, A. (2012). Progressive localism and the construction of political alternatives. *Transactions of the Institute of British Geographers, 37*(2), 177–182.

Glennon, R. (2017). *The death of improvement: An exploration of the legacy of performance and service improvement reform in English local authorities,*

1997–2017. Doctoral thesis for the award of PhD, Loughborough University.

Gray, M., & Barford, A. (2018). The depths of the cuts: The uneven geography of local government austerity. *Cambridge Journal of Regions, Economy and Society, 11*(3), 541–563.

Hackitt, J. (2018). *Building a safer future – Independent review of building Regulations and fire safety: Final report.* London: Ministry of Housing, Communities and Local Government.

HM Inspectorate of Constabulary and Fire & Rescue Services. (2017). *Proposed fire and rescue services inspection programme and framework 2018/19.* London: HM Inspectorate of Constabulary and Fire & Rescue Services.

HM Government. (2010). *The coalition: our programme for government. Freedom, fairness and responsibility.* Cabinet Office, London: TSO.

Home Office. (2016). *Home Secretary speech on fire reform.* Speech [Online]. Retrieved from https://www.gov.uk/government/speeches/home-secretary-speech-on-fire-reform. Accessed on July 26, 2019.

Home Office. (2017a). *Fire Minister's speech to reform.* Speech [Online]. Retrieved from https://www.gov.uk/government/speeches/fire-ministers-speech-to-reform. Accessed on July 26, 2019.

Home Office. (2017b). *Fire and rescue national framework for England government consultation.* London: The Stationery Office.

Home Office. (2018). *Fire and rescue national framework for England government.* London: The Stationery Office.

Hood, C. (1980). The politics of quangocide. *Policy & Politics*, *8*(3), 247–265(19).

Institute for Government. (2012). *Bonfire of the quangos*. Retrieved from https://www.instituteforgovernment.org.uk/news/latest/bonfire-quangos. Accessed on September 11, 2019.

Local Authorities Building Control. (2019). *Responding to MHCLG's consultation on the Hackitt review implementation*. London: Local Authorities Building Control.

Lowndes, V., & Pratchett, L. (2012). Local governance under the coalition government: Austerity, localism and the 'Big Society'. *Local Government Studies*, *38*(1), 21–40.

Lucas, I. (2015). *Independent cultural review of Essex county fire and rescue service*: Witham: Essex County Fire and Rescue Service.

May, T. (2016). *Home Secretary speech on fire reform*. London: Home Office.

Ministry of Housing, Communities and Local Government. (2019). *Building a safer future: Proposals for reform of the building safety regulation. A consultation*. London: The Stationery Office.

Murphy, P. (2019). *Opportunities spurned: a critical review of policy development, service delivery and public assurance in public services*. PhD, Nottingham: NTU.

Murphy, P., & Ferry, L. (2018). Another turn of the screw: Fire and rescue under the coalition government of 2010–2015. In P. Murphy & K. Greenhalgh (Eds.), *Fire and rescue services: Leadership and management perspectives* (pp. 45–60). Cham: Springer.

Murphy, P., & Greenhalgh, K. (2014a). Fire risk assessment – From property to people. *FIRE, 106*(1365), 37–39.

Murphy, P., & Greenhalgh, K. (2014b). Tenth anniversary of the 2004 Acts. *FIRE, 106*(1370), 14–16.

Murphy, P., & Greenhalgh, K. (2015). *Joint University research Group response to Home Office consultation: Enabling closer working between the emergency services.* Nottingham: Nottingham Trent University.

Murphy, P., & Greenhalgh, K. (Eds.). (2018a). *Fire and rescue services: Leadership and management perspectives.* Cham: Springer.

Murphy, P., & Greenhalgh, K. (2018b). The gathering storm: Modernisation, local alignment and collaboration. Fire and rescue services under the early new labour administrations from 1997 to 2005. In P. Murphy & K. Greenhalgh (Eds.), *Fire and rescue services: Leadership and management perspectives* (pp. 9–26). Cham: Springer.

Murphy, P., & Greenhalgh, K. (2018c). Consolidation and improvement. Fire and rescue under the new labour administrations 2005 – 2010. In P. Murphy & K. Greenhalgh (Eds.), *Fire and rescue services: Leadership and management perspectives* (pp. 27–44). Cham: Springer.

Murphy, P., Greenhalgh, K., Ferry, L., & Glennon, R. (2019). Fire and rescue services. In P. Murphy, L. Ferry, R. Glennon, & K. Greenhalgh (Eds.), *Public service accountability: Rekindling a debate* (pp. 107–126). Cham: Palgrave Macmillan.

Murphy, P., & Glennon, R. (2018). Governance reforms go off the boil. *FIRE*, Feb, pp. 31–33.

Murphy, P., & Lakoma, K. (2019). *Developing a model to facilitate evaluation of performance regimes and national frameworks.* Working Paper No 7, Nottingham Trent University, Nottingham.

Murphy, P., Lakoma, K., & Glennon, R. (2018). *A 'model' national framework for fire and rescue services in England.* Working Paper No 5. Nottingham Trent University, Nottingham.

Murphy, P., Wankhade, P., & Lakoma, K. (2019). The strategic and operational landscape of emergency services in the UK. *International Journal of Emergency Services.*

National Audit Office. (2015). *Financial sustainability of fire and rescue services.* London: National Audit Office.

O'Hara, M. (2015). *Austerity bites: A journey to the sharp end of cuts in the UK.* Bristol: Policy Press.

Office of the Deputy Prime Minister. (2004). *The fire and rescue service national framework 2004/05.* Wetherby: Office of the Deputy Prime Minister. Retrieved from http://webarchive.nationalarchives.gov.uk/20120919165309/http://www.communities.gov.uk/documents/fire/pdf/128923.pdf. Accessed on July 26, 2019.

Office of the Deputy Prime Minister. (2006a). *FSEC toolkit review manual.* London: The Stationery Office.

Office of the Deputy Prime Minister. (2006b). *The fire and rescue service national framework 2006/07.* London: Office of the Deputy Prime Minister. Retrieved from http://webarchive.nationalarchives.gov.uk/20120919165241/http://www.communities.gov.uk/documents/fire/pdf/144884.pdf. Accessed on July 26, 2019.

Packard, T., Patti, R., Daly, D., Tucker-Tatlow, J., & Farrell, C. (2007). Cutback management strategies. *Administration in Social Work*, *32*(1), 55–75.

Public Accounts Select Committee. (2016). *Financial sustainability of fire and rescue services inquiry. Twenty-third Report of Session 2015–16*. London: TSO

Raynsford, N. (2016). *Substance not spin: An insider's view of success and failure in government*. Bristol: Policy Press.

Schmidt, E., Groeneveld, S., & Van de Walle, S. (2017). A change management perspective on public sector cutback management: Towards a framework for analysis. *Public Management Review*, *19*(10), 1538–1555.

Spencer, T., Hayden, J., Murphy, P., & Glennon, R. (2019). Stating the obvious: Evaluating the state of public assurance in fire and rescue authorities in England. *International Journal of Emergency Services*, *8*(1), 20–33.

Travers, A., Amin-Smith, N., Murphy, P., & Whiteman, R. (2019). Oral evidence presented to the House of Commons committee on housing, Communities and Local Government investigating Local Government Finance and the 2019 Spending Review. Retrieved from http://data.parliament.uk/writtenevidence/committeeevidence.svc/evidencedocument/housing-communities-and-local-government-committee/local-government-finance-and-the-2019-spending-review/oral/102167.html. Accessed on June 04, 2019.

5

SO NEAR AND YET SO FAR: A RIGOROUS AND INDEPENDENT INSPECTORATE?

I intend to bring forward proposals to establish a rigorous and independent inspection regime for fire and rescue services in England.

(Rt Hon Theresa May MP 24th May 2016).

5.1 INTRODUCTION

This chapter analyses the antecedents, development and subsequent establishment of Her Majesty's Inspectorate of Constabulary and Fire & Rescue Services (HMICFRS) and the new inspection regime for Fire and Rescue Services in England, as established by the Policing and Crime Act 2017 (HMIC 2017; HMICFRS, 2018a). As the above quote suggests, the then Home Secretary, Theresa May, promised to put in place the right framework of institutions and processes to ensure operational integrity, as well as greater accountability and transparency for the fire service. She particularly highlighted the fact that 'there is no independent inspectorate; no regular audit of performance; and only limited available data on performance over time or between areas' (Home Office, 2016). This chapter examines the first of these inadequacies and the emergence of HMICFRS.

The following two sections present the history and antecedents of inspections in the police service, and in the fire and rescue services. We then examine and critically appraise HMICFRS and the new arrangements for inspection enshrined in the Fire and Rescue National Framework for England (Home Office, 2018) and in the Fire and Rescue Service Inspection Programme 2018/2019 (HMICFRS, 2018a). The final section draws out some lessons and recommendations for the future development of the inspectorate and its inspection regime.

5.2 THE HISTORY OF INSPECTION WITHIN POLICE SERVICES

Her Majesty's Inspectorate of Constabulary (HMIC) was one of the oldest inspectorates in the United Kingdom. It was established in 1856 by the County and Borough Police Act, which required every county and borough to maintain an 'efficient' police force. These forces were to be inspected annually by the newly created HMIC, with part of their central government grant dependent on the Inspectorate's report (Raine, 2008). As Cowley and Todd (2006) in their history of inspection explain, the first inspections were carried out and reports issued in 1857 and, perhaps not surprisingly, they highlighted significant variations between forces. This was not, however, a major concern to the government as policing at the time was considered primarily a local government matter. Nonetheless, a close relationship between the Home Office and the Inspectorate was established right from the start, although in the early days 'little central effort was devoted to co-ordinating the inspectors' activities or to developing national policy or to setting police standards' (Raine, 2008, p. 90).

It is interesting to note that during the late nineteenth century, in response to municipal parsimony and demonstrably overworked firefighters, proposals emerged in London, Liverpool and elsewhere to amalgamate police and fire-fighting forces. This was to allow reserves of police-firemen to supplement hard-pressed professional firefighters at times of emergencies. The 'police model', as it became known, faced sustained and widespread criticism not least from the Home Office's three inspectors of constabulary. The model was widely discredited following a particularly disastrous fire in a confectionary shop in Birmingham, where multiple fatalities were sustained through the incompetence of the police and their ignorance of basic rescue techniques and fire science. Subsequently the coroner forced the council to separate the police and fire departments (Ewen, 2010). As Ewen notes, it was around this time, following the Great Chicago fire of 1871, that American cities were also decoupling police and firefighters in order to establish independent professional fire brigades.

In their official history of the Inspectorate, Cowley and Todd (2006 p. 68) state:

> *While in its first 100 years the Inspectorate played a significant role as a reforming influence in policing, the depth and breadth of influence increased exponentially during the latter half of the 20th century. Policing itself evolved dramatically during this period and, strengthened by the introduction of Her Majesty's Chief Inspector* as the principal adviser to the Home Secretary, *the Inspectorate established itself as both a monitor of, and indeed a catalyst for, policing change.*

Following the 1962 Royal Commission on the police (HM Government, 1962) and the subsequent Police Act 1964, which introduced both a single system of police authorities and the tripartite policing arrangements shown in Table 5.1, there has been ever-greater central government control over the police.

Table 5.1. Key Responsibilities of the 'Tripartite' Policing Arrangements Established in 1964.

- **Home Secretary:** To promote the efficiency and effectiveness of the Police Service and to account to Parliament.
- **Police Authority:** To secure the maintenance of an efficient and effective police force in its area.
- **Chief Constable:** To direct and control the force.

Source: Cowley and Todd (2006).

The commission also recommended significant changes to the role of HMIC, which would henceforth have four duties:

1. To inspect each separate police force and report to the Home Secretary on its efficiency (as previously), but indicate any 'misgivings' they may have about the competence of the Chief Constable, including the manner in which he/she deals with complaints against the police.

2. To form an opinion about the adequacy of the provision made by the Police Authority and report any shortcomings to the Secretary of State.

3. To ensure that the results of central research are made available to all forces and to verify that new knowledge and up-to-date techniques are being applied.

4. To advise upon arrangements for promoting collaboration between forces and the development of ancillary services.

As a result, the inspectorate expanded and was regionalised. A Chief Inspector of Constabulary was appointed with a specific remit as the principal policing adviser to the Home Secretary. Assistant inspectors, administrative officers, researchers and specialist advisers were also appointed, in addition to more inspectors (Cowley & Todd, 2006).

Notably, the inspectorate developed a direct and very close relationship with the Home Office, epitomised by the establishment of the Home Office Police Research and Planning Branch in 1963, *under the direction* of the Chief Inspector. In addition, ministers played an increasingly active role in defining the inspectorate's work, as successive governments required the police to become more economical, efficient and effective and provide 'Best Value' for their services (Hale, Heaton, & Uglow, 2004; Raine, 2008). HMIC was closely involved in designing the measurement, management and monitoring tools and the assessment frameworks, and also assessed individual forces against these frameworks.

In line with the late twentieth century interest in accountability and much wider interpretations of this concept (Bovens, Schillemans, & Goodin, 2014; Sinclair, 1995), the HMIC's *modus operandi* gradually changed from a standards and compliance-based inspectorate to one that evaluated service and managerial performance. The key change came in 2003 when public service inspectorates became part of the 'inspection for improvement' regime of New Labour (Office of Public Services Reform, 2003a, 2003b). As Raine noted, 'HMIC reports... have been key to government's ability to shape the policing agenda' and to 'sharpening the whole basis of accountability in policing' (2008, p. 90).

5.3 THE PROPOSED CRIMINAL
JUSTICE INSPECTORATE

In 2006, following the Office for Public Service Reform report (OPSR was a policy unit in the Cabinet Office) and in order to try and improve public and managerial accountability by pooling experience and expertise, the government proposed a single inspectorate for Criminal Justice, Community Safety and Custody (Raine, 2008). It aimed to achieve this through the amalgamation of HMIC; Her Majesty's Inspectorate of Prisons, HM Inspectorate of Probation, HM Inspectorate of Court Administration and HM Crown Prosecution Inspectorate (Home Office, 2006). Encouraged by recent joint working between other watchdogs, and mirroring similar proposed 'super-inspectorate' amalgamations in Health and Social Care, in Children's Services and Education, and in the remainder of Local Governments' services, including Fire and Rescue Services (Davis & Martin, 2008), the government intended to 'join-up' inspection; to make inspection become more economic, efficient and effective, more community-focused and outcome-driven and to reduce the burden on those being inspected.

Amalgamation and rationalisation went ahead in the three other sectors, and the three lead inspectorates i.e. the Care Quality Commission, Audit Commission and Ofsted emerged with increased responsibilities and broader roles. However, the proposals for a single criminal justice inspectorate fell apart, partly because of the differences in purposes and values within the different inspectorates since their establishment. The inspectorates had doubts about whether a single inspectorate would have the ability to accommodate these differences and, ultimately, the proposals did not command sufficient cross-party political support (Raine, 2008). In particular, the logic of joining up local, community-based services to improve service delivery and outcomes in a particular area would appear anathema to a service such as prisons, whose primary purpose is to remove certain people from those communities. Although there was widespread agreement that the criminal justice system's inspectorates needed to work more collaboratively together (some more than others), it seemed that a single inspectorate was a step too far.

The financial recession, and the election in 2010 of a coalition government seeking to make substantial reductions in funding for public services led to the next major changes in police inspection and HMIC. In June 2012 the Home Secretary announced that Sir Tom Winsor, a lawyer and former Rail Regulator, would become the first civilian to become the Chief Inspector of Constabulary following the impending retirement of Sir Dennis O'Connor. Winsor had recently produced two reports for the government on police pay and conditions. Despite being unpopular with the Police Federation and rank and file officers, these reports were gratefully accepted and implemented by the government.

Sir Tom's appointment also followed the abolition of the National Police Improvement Agency, the introduction of Police and Crime Commissioners and changes to the role of the Association of Chief Police Officers. In his first major speech on taking office at the Royal United Services Institute (RUSI) Mr Winsor told his audience that preventing crime (rather than catching criminals) should be at the heart of good policing and that this approach would give the public more value for money (Travis, 2013).

New annual all-force assessments were announced in order to assess the effectiveness, efficiency and legitimacy of police services. The first of these reports, which were commonly known as PEEL assessments in reference to Sir Robert Peel (the prime minister who introduced the first police force in Britain), were published in November 2014. Theresa May's police reforms proved popular in her own party and initial assessments were encouraging (HM Chief Inspector of

Constabulary, 2015, 2016; Murphy, Ferry, & Glennon, 2019). This meant that when Mrs May finally acknowledged the need for a new inspectorate in Fire and Rescue Services (Home Office, 2016), she had a model conveniently to hand that, at least superficially, appeared to be fit for her purpose.

5.4 INSPECTION WITHIN FIRE AND RESCUE SERVICES

Although the First World War started a debate about the need for uniform or compatible operational standards in fire services, it wasn't until the Riverdale Committee on Fire Brigade Services (1936) and the subsequent Fire Brigades Act 1938, together with the rising threat of another war, that the fire service was propelled into national political debate. Fire-fighting arrangements became mandatory for local authorities (except county councils) and national inspection and an approved training school contributed towards delivering and monitoring efficiency and effectiveness (Ewen, 2010). The Second World War and the nationalisation of the fire service intervened, although a strong consensus emerged and persisted about the need for national standards, through which local resources would be deployed.

In 1947, the Fire Services Act denationalised the fire service. Policy responsibility was handed back to the Home Office, while service responsibility went back to local authorities. Although inspection and annual reporting had been announced in 1938, it was not until the 1947 Act that it was rolled out across the country as Her Majesty's Fire Service Inspectorate (HMFSI) was established and a new Chief Inspector appointed for England and Wales.

Afterwards, the political profile of the Fire Services declined over a long period – and this appeared to suit both the Home Office and the service itself (Murphy & Greenhalgh, 2018a). With the exception of industrial relations disputes and individual emergencies, the period was dominated by the traditional model of public administration in local government being applied to the fire service. The relationship to national policy making in the Home Office was widely characterised as 'benign neglect' (Murphy & Greenhalgh, 2013, 2018a; Raynsford, 2016) and the only primary legislation enacted was the Fire Services Act 1959. This largely dealt with pensions and staffing, and there was little secondary legislation or national policy guidance.

The inspectorate and the inspection regime were modelled on the arrangements for the police. Initially established as a strongly standards and compliance-based inspectorate that was influenced by wartime experiences, HMFSI slowly changed into a body that evaluated managerial performance as well as standards following the implementation of Best Value in 1999. However, the fire service never enjoyed as high a profile as the police, and HMFSI was never as close to its parent central government department as HMIC was to the Home Office. After the Audit Commission was established in 1983, Fire and Rescue Services (and the police) were included in the annual collection of performance data which complemented the Home Office Statistics. However, in the period up to 'modernisation' and the 2004 Fire and Rescue Services Act, the commission produced only two national reports on the fire service in nearly 20 years (Campbell-Smith, 2008).

The New Labour 'modernisation' of the Fire and Rescue Services was effectively initiated when Fire Services were designated Best Value organisations by the 1999 Local Government (Best Value) Act. A 'Best Value Inspectorate' had just been established within the Audit Commission to inspect the Best Value Reviews that local authorities had to provide under the terms of the Act, and HMFSI was initially designated as a Best Value Inspectorate (Home Office, 2000). Around this time the government commissioned the (highly critical) Burchill review on terms and conditions of service (2000) that was followed by the equally critical Bain review (2002), which took a wider look at the performance of fire services. These reports ultimately resulted in the Fire and Rescue Services Act of 2004, when Fire Services were re-designated Fire and Rescue Services to reflect wider responsibilities such as community safety and fire prevention as well as fire protection and incidence response. It also introduced the first national framework for the sector.

By the time that Bain reported in December 2002, the Audit Commission had been commissioned to develop and implement Comprehensive Performance Assessments for Local Authorities. In 2005 CPA was improved and expanded and included Fire and Rescue Services within its remit (Audit Commission, 2005). The government had also commissioned the Audit Commission, rather than HMFSI, to assess the progress that all services were making in implementing changes that fitted with the government's new strategy (Audit Commission, 2004a, 2004b).

The first fire service inspections did not address the operational parts of the service; instead, they focused on the performance of support functions and non-operational activities (Audit Commission, 2005; Murphy & Greenhalgh, 2013). HMFSI involvement in these inspections was limited, as it was in the design, development and implementation of the second CPA methodology for the service.

As mentioned above, the new 'inspection for improvement' regime of New Labour had started in 2003. At this point, Wendy Thompson, the former Head of the Best Value Inspectorate, became Director of the Office for Public Service Reform (OPSR) in the Cabinet Office. Thomson set out the government's intentions to rationalise Inspectorates and clarify their purpose (OPSR, 2003a, 2003b), and this led to the government proposing a single inspectorate for Criminal Justice, Community Safety and Custody (Home Office, 2006).

Notably, this new inspectorate did not include HMFSI. Instead, the fire service remained part of local government and various local authority inspectorates (which included the Housing Inspectorate, the Benefit Fraud Inspectorate and the Best Value Inspectorate, but excluded Children's' Services and Adult Social Services) were amalgamated and integrated in a single inspectorate under the leadership of the Audit Commission at around the same time (DCLG, 2006). The Audit Commission was also made responsible for co-ordinating the various inspection regimes, with an instruction to reduce bureaucracy and the impact of inspection on local services through better scheduling and co-ordination.

This process continued when the Department of Communities and Local Government created the role of Chief Fire and Rescue Adviser in 2007. At the same time, HMFSI was closed and the Audit Commission assumed responsibility for fire service inspections and carried out inspections and published CPA scores for fire and rescue services in 2006 and 2007. That year, the Local Government and Public Involvement in Health Act 2007 heralded a move to co-ordinated multi-organisational inspections of key public services within a single administrative area. These were known as Comprehensive Area Assessments (CAAs) and CAA replaced CPA in April 2009 (Audit Commission, 2009).

CAA assessed all key collaborations and partnership working in public services in an area. It focussed on Local Government, Health, the Police and the Fire and Rescue Services. It involved a corporate appraisal together with a 'use of resources' appraisal of each of these organisations. CAA provided individual organisational assessments of the local council, the local Primary Care Trust, the Police Constabulary and Police Authority and the Fire and Rescue Service and Authority. These were then combined into a Joint Inspectorate's Comprehensive Area Assessment and the area assessments and organisational assessments were published on a real-time publicly available dedicated website entitled 'One Place'.

While the financial recession and the election of a coalition government in 2010 had a big impact on the police service, it had an even greater impact on inspection within Fire and Rescue Services. Between 2007 and 2017 there was no dedicated independent inspectorate or inspectors for fire and rescue services. Between 2010 and 2017 there was no inspection at all, and in the summary report of the first tranche of new inspections HMICFRS acknowledge that "this is the first time in 12 years that the fire and rescue sector has been independently inspected" (HMICFRS, 2018b, p. 2).

5.5 THE NEW INSPECTORATE AND INSPECTION FRAMEWORK

Almost immediately on taking office after the general election in May 2010, the new Secretary of State at the Department of Communities and Local Government, Eric Pickles, announced the abolition of the Audit Commission and the termination of Comprehensive Area Assessments (DCLG, 2010a). Simultaneously, at the national Fire and Rescue conference in Harrogate, his Fire Minister Bob Neil announced a 'strategic review' of the fire and rescue sector and the government's role within it (DCLG, 2010b). He questioned whether or not a national framework was actually needed and announced the abandonment of various national targets including, most notably, equality and diversity targets. Austerity localism was to become the new policy approach (Featherstone, Ince, Mackinnon, Straus, & Cumbers, 2012; Lowndes & Pratchett, 2012); sector-led improvement and regulation and greater financial autonomy would be the means by which Fire and Rescue Services would deliver 'more for less' (DCLG, 2010b).

Early responses to the government's 'strategic review' assumed that some form of external inspection would have a role in the new performance management and assurance regime that would replace the unpopular annual universal assessments that were no longer considered cost-effective (Murphy & Greenhalgh, 2011). However, the 2012 National Framework (DCLG, 2012) made no provision for external inspection; instead it introduced a sector-led performance management system that relied on Peer Challenge, an Operational Assessments and accompanying Toolkit (Downe, Martin, & Doering, 2013, 2018; Kane, 2018; Murphy & Ferry, 2018; Murphy & Jones, 2016). This approach was popular with Fire and Rescue Services and over the first two years every Fire and Rescue Service undertook at least one peer assessment. This was a far higher level of engagement than in Local Government, where approximately 35% of authorities undertook a review in the first three years (LGA, 2019).

Fire Peer challenge and operational assessment undoubtedly helped Fire and Rescue Services confront the burgeoning task of improving services on a reducing resource base. Downe, Martin, and Doering (2018) provide an admirable account of both the strengths and the weaknesses of the approach from those who undertook reviews. The process and experience appeared to have many positive impacts, but it was also subject to considerable gaming in that services could choose which activities they put forward for review and could also influence who would be in their review team. Questions therefore persisted about whether peer challenge was sufficient on its own to ensure continuous improvement, maintenance of standards and public confidence in the service. Calls for the process to be complemented by an independent inspectorate (Murphy & Greenhalgh, 2014) were, perhaps surprisingly, strongly supported *inter alia* by the Fire Brigades Union (Wrack, 2016).

Indeed, the lack of an independent inspectorate was highlighted by both the National Audit Office report into the financial sustainability of fire and rescue services (NAO, 2015)

and by the subsequent Public Accounts Committee inquiry
based on the NAO report:

> *The lack of an independent inspectorate creates the risk
> that scrutiny of fire authorities will be inconsistent,
> and that oversight exercised by the Department will be
> incomplete.* Unlike other emergency services, there is no
> external inspection of fire and rescue services in
> England. While external challenge continues to be
> provided in the form of peer reviews organised by the
> sector itself, these are not designed to provide
> independent assurance to the Government, either on
> value for money or operational standards.
>
> (PAC, 2016, p. 7, emphasis in original).

In a speech to the reform think tank, Theresa May (the
Home Secretary between 2010 and 2016) was scathing about
her former colleagues' national framework and the peer
challenge system. She said that the fire service has 'succeeded
in spite of the framework it operates in, not because of it'. The
current system of review by peers, 'provides no assurance
whatsoever to the public because it allows chief fire officers to
set their own terms of reference, pick their own reviewer and
decide whether or not to publish the results. It is not so much
marking your own homework as setting your own exam
paper and resolving that you've passed – and it has to
change,'. She therefore intended to 'bring forward proposals
to establish a rigorous and independent inspection regime for
fire and rescue services in England' (Home Office, 2016).

After Mrs May became Prime Minister in July 2016, the
government included amendments to the draft Policing and
Crime Bill to ensure it would be reintroduced to Parliament
when it reconvened in September 2016. The Bill quickly
passed through the remaining parliamentary procedures;
received royal assent in January 2017 and duly came into

effect in April 2017 as the Policing and Crime Act (Murphy & Greenhalgh, 2018b).

In August 2016, the Home Office asked HMIC to prepare a scoping report and sought advice on operationalising the role of the new inspectorate. The alternatives of issuing a consultation or an open call for proposals; or commissioning a current or former Chief Fire Officer, or an existing Fire Inspectorate such as HM Fire Inspectorate Scotland, were rejected – if they were considered at all.

The initial scoping was therefore undertaken in 2016 by an ex-senior police officer and ex-HMIC inspector working under the guidance of Zoe Billingham, the HMIC Lead Inspector for the Eastern Region. Their report remains unpublished. However, subsequent discussions with the National Fire Chiefs Council and other stakeholders confirm that the Home Office subsequently considered only two potential bodies to develop the new inspection regime. HMIC was one and the other was 'Blue Light Works', a collaborative partnership who had previously worked on digital technology with the Police and the Home Office (Murphy, 2017).

In a speech on 7 February 2017, immediately after the Policing and Crime Act 2017 received royal assent, Brandon Lewis MP, appointed by Theresa May in June 2016 as the Home Office Minister for Policing and the Fire Service, announced further information about the new inspectorate (Home Office, 2017a). He said that a new 'suitable' inspectorate would be modelled on HMIC with its emphasis on efficiency and effectiveness. It would have the power to undertake joint inspections with HMIC, as well as thematic inspections (inspections of a particular activity or responsibility), service inspections and organisational inspections. He also said that it was 'essential that regardless of provider, inspection teams include suitable skills and expertise from the fire sector'. Bearing these principles in mind, it was perhaps unsurprising that the government gave HMIC responsibility for fire and rescue services' inspections, renaming it HM Inspectorate of Constabulary and Fire & Rescue Services (HMICFRS) on 19 July 2017, the day before the summer recess of parliament.

In September 2017, the latest version of the PEEL police inspection programme was published and on 19 December 2017 the proposed fire and rescue services inspection programme and framework for 2018/2019 were published for public consultation. Taking the Christmas and New Year break into account this allowed for the minimum 30 working days for a consultation that closed on 19th February 2018. Despite ministerial assurances on transparency and responsiveness, the following statement gives a more accurate impression of how open, transparent and responsive the new Inspectorate intended to be:

> *Following the close of the consultation on 19th February 2018, HM Chief Inspector of Fire & Rescue Services will consider respondents' views and, if he determines it appropriate to do so, change the proposed inspection programme and framework before putting it to the Home Secretary for approval.*
> (HMICFRS 2017 p1).

According to HMICFRS, there were more than 65 responses to the consultation, although neither their contents nor any analysis of them were published. The initial response from HMICFRS to the consultation is shown in Table 5.2, which highlights the changes made in the finalised framework. This shows that minor wording changes were made to just six paragraphs, none of them in any way substantial or meaningful. The consultation could reasonably be considered a waste of time and, because most respondents were either fire and rescue services or other publicly funded bodies, it was also a considerable waste of public money. The revised wording

Table 5.2. Changes Resulting from the Formal Consultation.

Consultation	Inspection Programme and Framework
Foreword, p. 3 We have given prominence to the following principal themes: (…) • The ability of the service to train staff, embrace diversity and develop a positive working culture	**Foreword, p. 3** We have chosen to focus on these main themes: (…) • The ability of the service to train staff, embrace diversity and develop a positive working culture **to reflect the level of public and professional interest.**
Introduction, p. 6 **HMICFRS'** assessments are designed to enable the public to see how each fire and rescue service's performance changes over time and **in relation to the performance of other services.**	**Introduction, p. 5** **Our** assessments are designed to enable the public to see how each fire and rescue service's performance changes over time and **compared with the performance of other services.**
Inspecting governance arrangements, p. 7 If during an inspection we identify evidence that the decisions and activities of those within the fire and rescue authority, police, fire and crime commissioner, locally elected mayors and, in London, the Mayor's Office inhibit the efficiency and effectiveness of the chief fire officer, we may carry out a separate corporate governance inspection.	**Inspecting governance arrangements, p. 7** In some circumstances, we may carry out a separate corporate governance inspection. We would do this if an inspection indicates that the efficiency and effectiveness of the chief fire officer is inhibited by the decisions and activities of those within the fire and rescue authority, the police, fire and crime commissioner, locally elected mayors and, in London, the Mayor's Office. We will develop a methodology for the corporate governance inspection and will consult on this in due course.

Table 5.2. (Continued)

Consultation	Inspection Programme and Framework
Professional standards body, p. 12 Part of the Home Office reform programme for fire and rescue services **is the formation of a professional standards body.** It is currently in development.	**Professional standards body, p. 11** Part of the Home Office's fire reform **programme is to develop a coherent and comprehensive set of professional standards** for all areas of fire and rescue services' work, **drawing on existing standards where appropriate.**
Advisory and reference groups, p. 13 **The HMICFRS Fire Technical Advisory Group** considers how to develop appropriate methods of data collection and analysis to support the inspection methodology. The members of **the Fire Technical Advisory Group** include representatives of the National Fire Chiefs Council co-ordinating committees, the Home Office, representative bodies, fire and rescue services and others. **It will also include representatives from the professional standards body, when it has been established.**	**Advisory and reference groups, p. 12** **Our fire technical advisory group** considers how to develop appropriate methods of data collection and analysis to support the inspection methodology. The members of **this group** include representatives of the National Fire Chiefs Council co-ordinating Committees, the Home Office and fire and rescue services.

Source: Authors compiled from HMICFRS (2017, 2018a).

merely reinforced the Chief Inspector's initial views as to how inspections should proceed, as expressed in the draft published for consultation.

5.6 THE NEW INSPECTORATE AND INSPECTION FRAMEWORK – RIGOROUS? COMPREHENSIVE? FIT FOR PURPOSE?

Responses to consultation focussed on three significant inadequacies all of which are reflected in the public assurance domain of the model:

1. The scope and rigour of the proposed inspections,

2. The adequacy of the evidence on which judgements will be made,

3. The extent of 'independence' within the system.

In order to achieve a rigorous inspection, one might have assumed (as our model suggests) that all of the services provided by the Fire Authority, together with the performance of the Fire Authority, itself would be part of the assessment. This is not the case. In addition, both the draft consultation and the final framework make clear that the inspections 'will not include an assessment of corporate governance or the accountability structures'. The framework clarifies that HMICFRS's judgements depend on policy, practice and performance, yet neither the primary policy-making body (the authority, which is responsible for assessing strategic risks, determining strategic priorities, establishing the budget and ensuring public safety), nor the principal scrutiny or accountability arrangements, will be routinely and regularly assessed.

Chapter 3 highlighted the lack of evidence on which inspectors are able to base their judgements. Compounding this issue, it is notable that the framework will not assess all services and activities. For example, where the governing body (i.e. the Fire Authority or the PFCC), has decided to outsource activities or services to public, private or voluntary providers, or to joint delivery partnerships or collaborations, these functions are not covered by the inspections (HMICFRS, 2018a).

In the case of collaborations, the first inspections only examined collaborations with the other blue light services (ambulance and police). They did not assess Fire and Rescue Services' contribution to wider issues such as public health and social outcomes, or partnership such as that with local authorities, other than the local resilience forum. The proposed approach, content and questions were therefore too narrow to provide 'rounded' and comprehensive comparable judgements.

Nevertheless, there are some very clear findings and messages from the reports of the first two tranches of inspections of 30 services (HMICFRS, 2018b, 2019). These suggest significant variation in standards, services and levels of risk across the country and point out that the data and intelligence available for planning and delivery is inconsistent and inadequate. People management is generally poor; staff do not feel valued or supported and often have to endure organisational cultures and poor leadership (HMICFRS, 2018b; HMICFRS, 2019). Sustained reductions in resources mean that there are a number of services in need of improvement, and very few pockets of excellence. Financially, a number of services have insufficient resources to meet current expectations, and yet they are facing further reductions in their budgets (HMICFRS, 2018b; ONS, 2019). Fire regulation and enforcement; and prevention and protection services more generally, have been deprioritised and increasingly under-resourced contrary to national and local policy (HMICFRS, 2018b; ONS, 2019;

Home Office, 2019). This view is shared by the Fire Brigades Union:

> *HMICFRS is absolutely right, a decade and a half of localism and austerity has led to fragmented services and a postcode lottery of response times and crewing levels, leaving the public dangerously unsafe in some areas.*
> (Matt Wrack, FBU General Secretary 2019).

A final issue left unaddressed relates to the extent of independence of both the inspectorate itself and the inspections it will undertake. Unlike in Scotland, independence from government and from the service itself is not guaranteed by statute. HMICFRS currently has its budget and financing determined by the government through the Home Office, rather than being set by parliament or by an appropriate independent process. In operationalising its activities, the inspectorate, as is hardly surprising given its antecedents and genesis in the former HMIC, appears to be located closer to the executive rather than to the scrutiny of government and public service through parliamentary and non-parliamentary processes.

To give one example, the annual inspection programme of regular service inspections has to be approved in advance by the Home Office. The inspectorate claims 'no minister, police and crime commissioner or fire authority can interfere with the contents of an HMICFRS report or the judgement of HM Inspectors', (HMICFRS, 2018c) which is true, but the Policing and Crime Act 2017 gives the Home Secretary the power to specify, scope and mandate either thematic or individual inspections (Home Office, 2017b). According to the website neither the current Chief Inspector nor any of the board has a background or experience in Fire and Rescue Services, (HMICFRS, 2018c) and inspections appear to rely heavily on staff seconded from local fire and rescue services (HMICFRS, 2018d).

One has to question whether this is the level of independence that Mrs May implied when promising to reinstate a robust and independent Inspectorate. Whether this is a broken promise or an empty promise depends to a certain extent upon how the inspectorate develops, and whether it can build in more independence as it grows and matures. In its current form it is not yet fit for purpose and in our view falls short of what the public and the service expected when they supported the re-creation of a modern independent inspectorate for the Fire and Rescue Services (HMICFRS, 2018d).

5.7 CONCLUSIONS

In summary, we would argue that the new inspectorate falls short of meeting the expectations of the assurance pillar of our model and the standards set out by Mrs May when announcing its creation. As we have outlined, there are several reasons for this. First, the HMICFRS claims to independence for the organisation and the emerging process are clearly contestable and have not always been in accordance with the Nolan principles. The development of the policy and the inspectorate has been based on an ambiguous and/or unrealistic vision and strategic intent for the service, built on an inadequate evidence base and a flawed and limited consultation process. Second, the new inspectorate the national framework and initial programme of inspections do not, as yet, provide the key stakeholders (including the public and the Fire and Rescue Services) with the level and quality of assurance they would normally expect from a public service. Third, the inspections themselves have highlighted inconsistencies, inadequacies and omissions in the evidence available at the local level that are comparable with those that we identified at the national level in Chapter 3. They acknowledge the establishment of the new standards board but note that to-date there have been no outcomes to this process – either in terms of professional standards or performance standards. Fourth, the inspectorates concern for unwarranted variation in systems, processes, standards and quality assurance across local services reflects the inadequacy of internal and external scrutiny and the previous Fire Peer Challenge and Operational Assessment system derided by Mrs May and her ministers. It also reflects systematic inadequacies in both policy and leadership at the national and local levels.

This overall picture suggests that political expediency and speed of delivery may have been prioritised ahead of improving services, public safety and assurance to the public in the latest performance regime. In its current state of development our model suggests this is clearly a sub-optimal regime with identifiable areas for further improvement, albeit one that is clearly an improvement on its predecessor.

REFERENCES

Audit Commission. (2004a). *Verification of the progress on modernisation: Fire and rescue services in England and Wales*. London: Audit Commission.

Audit Commission. (2004b). *Second verification report on the progress on modernisation: Fire and rescue services in England and Wales*. London: Audit Commission.

Audit Commission. (2005). *Comprehensive performance assessment: Learning from CPA for the fire and rescue service in England 2005*. London: Audit Commission.

Audit Commission. (2009). *Comprehensive area assessment framework document*. London: Audit Commission.

Bain, G., Lyons, M., & Young, M. (2002). *The future of the fire service: Reducing risk, saving lives: The independent review of the fire service*. Norwich: The Stationery Office.

Bovens, M., Schillemans, T., & Goodin, R. (Eds.). (2014). Public accountability. In *The Oxford handbook of public accountability* (pp. 1–22). Oxford: Oxford University Press.

Burchill, F. (2000). *Report of the independent inquiry into the machinery for determining firefighters' conditions of service*. London: Her Majesty's Stationery Office.

Campbell-Smith, D. (2008). *Follow the money: A history of the audit commission*. London: Penguin.

Cowley, R., & Todd, P. (2006). *The history of Her Majesty's Inspectorate of Constabulary: The first 150 years, 1856–2006*. London: Her Majesty's Inspectorate of Constabulary.

Davis, H., & Martin, S. (Eds.). (2008). *Public services inspection in the UK*. London: Jessica Kingsley Publishers.

Department of Communities and Local Government. (2006). *Strong and prosperous communities: The local government white paper (Vols. 1 & 2)*. London: The Stationery Office.

Department of Communities and Local Government. (2010a). *Eric Pickles to disband Audit Commission in new era of town hall transparency*. Announcement as a news item 25th June 2010 that the Secretary of State had written instructing the Audit Commission to terminate CAA. Retrieved from https://www.gov.uk/government/news/eric-pickles-to-disband-audit-commission-in-new-era-of-town-hall-transparency. Accessed on October 31, 2019.

Department of Communities and Local Government. (2010b). *Leading a lean and efficient fire and rescue service*. Fire Minister Bob Neill's speech to Fire and Rescue 2010 Conference, Harrogate, England.

Department of Communities and Local Government. (2012). *Fire and rescue national framework for England*. London: The Stationery Office.

Downe, J., Martin, S. J., & Doering, H. (2013). *Supporting councils to succeed: Independent evaluation of the LGA's corporate peer challenge programme*. London: Local Government Association.

Downe, J., Martin, S. J., & Doering, H. (2018). Peer challenge: A sector-led approach to performance improvement in fire and rescue services. In P. Murphy & K. Greenhalgh (Eds.), *Fire and rescue services: Leadership and management perspectives* (pp. 61–76). London: Springer.

Ewen, S. (2010). *Fighting fires: Creating the British fire service 1800–1978*. Basingstoke: Palgrave Macmillan.

Featherstone, D., Ince, A., Mackinnon, D., Straus, K., & Cumbers, A. (2012). Progressive localism and the construction of political alternatives. *Transactions of the Institute of British Geographers, 37*(2), 177–182.

Hale, C., Heaton, R., & Uglow, S. (2004). Uniform styles? Aspects of police centralization in England and Wales. *Policing and Society, 14*(4), 291–312.

HM Chief Inspector of Constabulary. (2015). *State of policing 2014: The annual assessment of policing in England and Wales her Majesty's Chief Inspector of Constabulary*. London: Her Majesty's Inspectorate of Constabulary.

HM Chief Inspector of Constabulary. (2016). *State of policing 2015: The annual assessment of policing in England and Wales*. London: Her Majesty's Inspectorate of Constabulary.

HM Government. (1962). *Final report of the royal commission on the police (the Willink report) Cmd 1728*. London: The Stationery Office.

HM Inspectorate of Constabulary. (2017). *Inspection programme and framework 2017/18*. London: Her Majesty's Inspectorate of Constabulary.

HM Inspectorate of Constabulary and Fire & Rescue Services. (2017). *Proposed fire and rescue services inspection programme and framework 2018/19 for consultation*. London: HM Inspectorate of Constabulary and Fire & Rescue Services.

HM Inspectorate of Constabulary and Fire & Rescue Services. (2018a). *Fire and rescue services inspection programme and framework 2018/19*. London: HM Inspectorate of Constabulary and Fire & Rescue Services.

HM Inspectorate of Constabulary and Fire & Rescue Services. (2018b). *Fire and rescue service inspections 2018/19 summary of findings from Tranche 1*. London: HM Inspectorate of Constabulary and Fire & Rescue Services.

HM Inspectorate of Constabulary and Fire & Rescue Services. (2018c). *About us*. Retrieved from https://www.justice inspectorates.gov.uk/hmicfrs/about-us/. Accessed on December 5, 2019.

HM Inspectorate of Constabulary and Fire & Rescue Services. (2018d). *Further information short term secondments*. Retrieved from https://www.justiceinspectorates.gov.uk/ hmicfrs/about-us/working-at-hmicfrs/short-term-secondee-programme/further-information-short-term-secondments/. Accessed on December 5, 2019.

HM Inspectorate of Constabulary and Fire & Rescue Services. (2019). *Fire and rescue service 2018/19 summary of findings from Tranche 2*. London: HM Inspectorate of Constabulary and Fire & Rescue Services.

Home Office. (2000). *Report of Her Majesty's Chief Inspector of fire services for England and Wales 1999/00*. London: Home Office.

Home Office. (2006). *A single inspectorate for justice and community safety*. London: Home Office.

Home Office. (2016). *Home Secretary speech on fire reform*. Speech [Online]. Retrieved from https://www.gov.uk/government/speeches/home-secretary-speech-on-fire-reform. Accessed on October 31, 2019.

Home Office. (2017a). *Fire Minister's speech to reform*. Speech [Online]. Retrieved from https://www.gov.uk/government/speeches/fire-ministers-speech-to-reform. Accessed on October 31, 2019.

Home Office. (2017b). *Inspection of fire and rescue authorities in England: Written statement - HCWS78 home secretary 19 July 2017*. London: HCWS78.

Home Office. (2018). *Fire and rescue national framework for England*. London: Home Office.

Home Office. (2019). *Fire prevention & protection statistics*, England, April 2018 to March 2019. Retrieved from https://assets.publishing.service.gov.uk/government/uploads/system/uploads/attachment_data/file/836909/fire-prevention-protection-1819-hosb2319.pdf. Accessed on December 5, 2019.

Kane, E. (2018). Collaboration in the emergency services. In P. Murphy & K. Greenhalgh (Eds.), *Fire and rescue services: Leadership and management perspectives* (pp. 77–92). London: Springer.

Local Government Association. (2019). *Outcomes: Peer challenge reports.* Retrieved from https://www.local.gov.uk/our-support/peer-challenges/peer-challenges-we-offer/corporate-peer-challenges/outcomes-peer. Accessed on August 20, 2019.

Lowndes, V., & Pratchett, L. (2012). Local governance under the coalition government: Austerity, localism and the big society. *Local Government Studies, 38*(1), 21–40.

Murphy, P. (2017). Independent inspectorate in danger of becoming Home Office handmaiden. *FIRE, 112*(1398), 9–11.

Murphy, P., & Ferry, L. (2018). Another turn of the screw: Fire and rescue under the coalition government of 2010–2015. In P. Murphy & K. Greenhalgh (Eds.), *Fire and rescue services: Leadership and management perspectives* (pp. 45–59). London: Springer.

Murphy, P., Ferry, L., & Glennon, R. (2019). Police. In P. Murphy, L. Ferry, R. Glennon, & K. Greenhalgh (Eds.), *Public service accountability: Rekindling a debate* (pp. 91–105). Cham: Palgrave Macmillan.

Murphy, P., & Greenhalgh, K. (2011). Strategic review offers unique opportunity. *FIRE*, January, pp. 34–35.

Murphy, P., & Greenhalgh, K. (2013). Performance management in fire and rescue services. *Public Money & Management, 33* (3), 225–232.

Murphy, P., & Greenhalgh, K. (2014). Peer challenge needs an independent Fire Inspectorate. *FIRE*, July/August, pp. 17–19.

Murphy, P., & Greenhalgh, K. (2018a). Introduction. In P. Murphy & K. Greenhalgh (Eds.), *Fire and rescue services: Leadership and management perspectives* (pp. 1–8). London: Springer.

Murphy, P., & Greenhalgh, K. (2018b). 2016 and the future: Changing the governance paradigm and the operating environment if not the financial context. In P. Murphy & K. Greenhalgh (Eds.), *Fire and rescue services: Leadership and management perspectives* (pp. 227–235). London: Springer.

Murphy, P., & Jones, M. (2016). Building the next model for intervention and turnaround in poorly performing local authorities in England. *Local Government Studies, 42*(5), 698–716.

National Audit Office. (2015). *Financial sustainability of fire and rescue services, HC 491*. London: National Audit Office.

Office for National Statistics. (2019). *Activities, spending and productivity in the fire and rescue services since 2009.* Released 30 May 2019. Retrieved from https://www.ons.gov.uk/economy/governmentpublicsectorandtaxes/publicspending/articles/activitiesspendingandproductivityinthefireandrescueservicessince2009/2019-05-30. Accessed on December 5, 2019.

Office of Public Services Reform. (2003a). *Inspecting for improvement: Developing a customer focused approach.* London: Cabinet Office.

Office of Public Services Reform. (2003b). *The government's policy on Inspection of Public Services.* London: Cabinet Office.

Public Accounts Committee. (2016). *Financial sustainability of fire and rescue services: Twenty-third report of session 2015–16.* London: The Stationery Office.

Raine, J. W. (2008). Inspection and the criminal justice agencies. In H. Davis & S. Martin (Eds.), *Public services inspection in the UK* (pp. 87–101). London: Jessica Kingsley Publishers.

Raynsford, N. (2016). This won't take too much of your time. In *Substance not spin: An insider's view of success and failure in government*. Bristol: Policy Press.

Riverdale. (1936). *Departmental Committee on Fire Brigade Services, Cmd 5224*. London: The Stationery Office.

Sinclair, A. (1995). The chameleon of accountability: Forms and discourses. *Accounting, Organizations and Society, 20*(2–3), 219–237.

Travis, A. (2013). Police 'should focus more on preventing crime than catching criminals' *Guardian Newspaper*, Home Affairs Editor 29 April 2013. Retrieved from https://www.theguardian.com/uk/2013/apr/29/police-focus-crime-catching-criminals. Accessed on December 5, 2019.

Wrack, M. (2016). *FBU reacts to Theresa May's first speech on the fire and rescue service* [Online]. Retrieved from https://www.fbu.org.uk/news/2016/05/24/fbu-reacts-theresa-mays-first-speech-fire-and-rescue-service   Accessed   on October 14, 2018.

Wrack, M. (2019). *HMICFRS report confirms dangerous fire service fragmentation*. Retrieved from https://www.fbu.org.uk/news/2019/06/20/hmicfrs-report-confirms-dangerous-fire-service-fragmentation. Accessed on October 31, 2019.

6

A GLASS HALF-EMPTY
OR A GLASS HALF-FULL?:
CONCLUSIONS, REFLECTIONS
AND REACTIONS

6.1 INTRODUCTION

This book has critically reviewed the government's attempts to rebuild the performance management regime of the fire and rescue services in England over the last four years. It has focussed in particular on the three areas that Theresa May identified as the crux of the problem in her last speech as Home Secretary before becoming Prime Minister, specifically that there was 'no independent inspectorate; no regular audit of performance; and only limited available data' (May, 2016, p. 8).

During the course of this book, we have applied the evaluative model outlined in Chapter 2 to each of the three areas (Chapters 3–5). This concluding chapter summarises and reflects upon the conclusions from those previous chapters and, in the spirit of an 'Emerald Points' publication, suggests some potential reactions that we believe would help to improve the current regime in all three of the key areas of policy development, service delivery and public assurance.

6.2 BACKGROUND

On 31 March 2015, the Audit Commission formally closed its doors and relinquished responsibility for oversight of the fire and rescue service, then under the stewardship of the former Department of Communities and Local Government (DCLG) and Secretary of State Eric Pickles. This responsibility passed to the National Audit Office (NAO). In anticipation of this transfer in February 2015, the NAO commissioned a report on the financial sustainability, accountability and transparency of the four main locally delivered public services that were due to be transferred i.e. local government, health, police and fire and rescue services (Ferry & Murphy, 2015; Murphy, Ferry, Glennon, & Greenhalgh, 2019a). Shortly after this report was delivered, the NAO commissioned a further report and advice specifically on the fire and rescue service (Murphy, 2015a, 2015b), which was highly critical of DCLG's apparent disinterest in how well the service was operating (NAO, 2015). In January 2016, the government announced that responsibility for the service would be transferred from the DCLG to the Home Office from whence it had come in 2001. This did not, however, deter the Public Accounts Select Committee from undertaking its own review of the service based upon the NAO report. The committee issued an equally uncompromising and highly critical review (PAC, 2016), that led to Theresa May's reaction. Her response was to propose a set of reforms that were clearly based on the reforms to the police that she had overseen between 2010 and 2015. They included adding amendments to the legislation then in its final stages in parliament, which emerged as Chapters 1–4 of the Policing and Crime Act 2017. Chapters 1–4 of the Act made the replacement of the 2012 national framework and the creation of a new inspectorate inevitable and highlighted the need for significant improvement in the data and information available for policy development, service delivery and public assurance.

6.3 CONCLUSIONS

There has been a long-stated attachment and apparently strong adherence to evidence-based policy and service configuration (Ewen, 2010). Yet, the evidential basis for decision-making in fire and rescue services, whether for policy-making, service delivery or for assurance purposes at both the national and local levels has been clearly inadequate and was already showing signs of significantly deterioration in 2015/2016, when the NAO and PAC produced their reports (Murphy et al., 2019a). Chapter 3 demonstrates how little improvement has been made since that time. The recent inspections of local services have to date merely confirmed that the local evidence base is inadequate just as the NAO report demonstrated inadequacy at the national level. The inspections have noted the increasing variation in the evidence used by local services, while the NFCC has instigated a review of the wide variety of community risk methodologies being used (NFCC, 2017); others have also pointed out that the current inspection processes do not capture the adequacy of the Integrated Risk Management Plans, which underpin all service configurations and deployments (Murphy, Lakoma, & Toothill, 2019b).

Chapter 3 sought to identify which parts or areas of the collective evidence base are inadequate or, in some cases, even absent. It examined the five different areas where data and information are essential and identified those areas that were well served and those areas that were not so well served. It found that even the strongest area ('response services') has data and analytical capacity gaps at both national and local levels. Protection and prevention services and, to a lesser extent, corporate and management services and the support for collaboration, reveal much greater gaps or inadequacies in their data and intelligence.

The Fire and Rescue Sector is not particularly large, nor is the range of services it provides overly complex; thus data collection and the evidence required for its performance regime is not extensive. However, it does need to be rigorously quality assured at both national and local levels and this makes the slow progress in establishing the new Standards Board particularly disappointing.

There is also considerable overlap in the evidence required at both national and local levels and in the three domains of policy, service delivery and assurance. This suggests that the need for improved data and information could be relatively quickly and efficiently addressed provided there is genuine co-operation and collaboration across the 'community of interest' and a relatively modest increase in dedicated resources. It is equally apparent that a considerable amount of these data needs to be consistent across all fire and rescue services and that the most economic, efficient and effective way to achieve this consistency is at the national level. It, therefore, requires strategic alignment, co-responsibility and co-production. All have been notably absent over the last four years.

When we have applied the typology of performance management regimes outlined in Chapter 3, it becomes clear that, both nationally and locally, fire and rescue services are currently having to contend with a 'data-poor' operating environment. We show how all relevant actors – the government, the inspectorate and the wider community of interest – recognise this problem; yet the solution requires a collaborative and co-productive approach to produce it and this is not happening or is not happening quickly enough.

Chapter 4 provides a short comparative review of each of the first four national frameworks (ODPM, 2004, 2006; DCLG, 2008, 2012), before looking in more detail at the current 2018 National Framework (Home Office, 2018). The overall purpose of the chapter is similar to that of Chapters 3 and 5 in that it seeks to identify or illustrate which parts of the current framework are inadequate or in need of future improvement and what, if anything, is missing. To do this, we have employed our evaluative model set out in Chapter 2.

This analysis has immediately highlighted the importance of the situational or contextual constraints around the fire and rescue service, because the legislative basis, the resources available to the sector and the strategic and operational organisational landscape had all significantly changed, or were due to change, since the previous framework in 2012. These factors have had significant implications for all three domains of policy development, service delivery and assurance to the public. However, despite commitments to implement recommendations arising out of the Grenfell Inquiry and the Hackitt Review (2017), there would be no extra resources as the framework echoed the 2017 spending review which had reconfirmed a constantly diminishing resource envelope up until 2022. The overall conclusion in Chapter 3 was that the 2018 framework was more appropriate than the 2012 framework, but that is hardly surprising given the changing context and the manifest inadequacies of the 2012 arrangements.

Chapter 4 found that the 2018 Framework reiterated three key pillars and/or objectives of the service, i.e. FRSs had to identify, analyse and articulate risks in IRMPs, give greater priority to prevention and protection services, and provide greater accountability to local communities and the public. This was despite the prevention and protection having been deprioritised in practice and accountability clearly deteriorating in both policy and practice between 2012 and 2018.

The 2018 framework also included two 'additional' objectives: improved collaboration between the three blue light emergency services, as required by Chapter 1 of the 2017 Act, and the development of a resilient, skilled, flexible and diverse workforce. Both of these made the objectives of the framework more comprehensive than its immediate predecessor although not as comprehensive as the 2006 and 2008 frameworks.

The overall conclusions of Chapter 4 are alluded to in the title of the chapter. Whilst the framework is an improvement on the 2012 edition, it is also not as good as it could have been if the lessons from previous frameworks had been adequately learnt. Similarly, in retrospect, it is becoming clear that the government has pulled back somewhat from the resolute position announced by Theresa May and her ministers in 2016 and 2017. The current strategic intent of the government is neither clear nor consistent. The new duty to collaborate has been limited to the three emergency services and attempts to align the organisational landscape and the policy-delivery-assurance regimes have been only partially successful. In practice, the 2018 framework represents a case of two steps forward, one step back in all three of its key components.

The third component was the establishment of rigorous and independent external inspection arrangements. These would seek to drive improvement and provide the government and the public with greater accountability, transparency and assurance around the performance of the services. Chapter 5, therefore, follows the pattern established in Chapters 3 and 4 in attempting to identify those aspects of the inspectorate and its inspections that are in need of future improvement and what may be missing.

The broad conclusions of Chapter 5 are in some ways very similar to those in Chapters 3 and 4. Given that there was no dedicated external inspection for almost a decade prior to 2017 (sector-led improvement unfortunately preferred to use a relatively poor system of peer review), the creation of HMICFRS was almost bound to be a 'step forward' at least in terms of improved assurance. However, as Chapter 5 demonstrates, it is neither good enough nor as good as it could have been. At least in part, a narrowly homogenous set of views appear to have been taken into account during its development and strategic positioning – namely those of HMIC and not other, previous and current inspectorates.

In terms of the role, remit and strategic positioning of the inspectorate, it falls short of what the public deserves and the services expected when they supported the re-creation of a modern, independent inspectorate for the Fire and Rescue Services. It also falls short of meeting the expectations of the assurance pillar of the evaluative model and finally, it fails the standards set out by Teresa May when she announced its creation. Its relationship to both government and parliament needs urgent reconsidering, as claims of robust independence for the organisation and the emerging process are clearly contestable (Murphy, 2017). The development of inspection policy and the inspectorate have been based on an ambiguous and unrealistic vision for a service that is operating with inadequate resources and is currently reliant on an (acknowledged) unreliable evidence base. Policy-makers have been overly influenced by the (former) HMIC's model for inspecting policing rather than existing or previous fire service inspections in the United Kingdom, or elsewhere; we contend that the two services are sufficiently different to warrant a more bespoke inspectorate.

The inspections are clearly not comprehensive, given that they 'do not include an assessment of corporate governance or the accountability structures' (HMICFRS, 2018, p. 5), include only some of the key stakeholder collaborations and do not extend to outsourced services. Again, local weaknesses in the evidence base are matched by national ones, as previous reports have identified.

6.4 REFLECTIONS

It is possible to view the government's attempts to rebuild the performance management regime of the fire and rescue services in England over the last four years either positively or negatively. Is it a glass-half-full or a glass-half-empty? Perhaps a more suitable metaphor that emerges from this study is that it is a bit of a 'curate's egg'; we have attempted to give credit for the improvements but cannot shy away from highlighting the inadequacies that remain.

Theresa May's vision of a new and revitalised performance management regime based on better data, a renewed purpose, and with better governance and accountability has lost a lot of its shine and momentum. Perhaps we were unduly optimistic about her commitment to the fire service and her own leadership and managerial competence, even though her claims to have reformed the police have recently been challenged by the Police Foundations' launch of their Strategic Review of Policing in England and Wales (The Police Foundation, 2019). As Chapter 4 demonstrates, there is a new national framework that is a great improvement on the 2012 framework, but it is not comprehensive and its implementation has been slow, half-hearted and, at times, incoherent.

For example, it is interesting that governance and accountability are two of the things that needed improving but neither is in the inspection methodology. The former HMIC and HMICFRS have been required since the 1964 Police Act to form an opinion about the adequacy of the police authority governance, but governance and accountability were explicitly excluded from the first round of fire inspections. Similarly, there is a new, dedicated inspectorate, albeit within an organisation with two asymmetric branches, where fire is firmly the junior partner.

HMICFRS did adopt a sensibly cautious and pragmatic approach to the first inspections, which carefully balanced the differing expectations of their varied audiences: the government, the public, stakeholders and partners as well as the services themselves, their staff and the media. The inspectorate needed to justify the government's investment in the new regime, provide clear and fair assessments (as far as their methodology would allow them to), and articulate robust messages in their role of 'speaking truth to power'. It is clear from our study that the next round of inspections needs a much broader scope, an improved methodology, and more and better data to work with. Data and information, or the content, quality and process of IRMPs, would make an interesting subject for the themed inspections lauded by the government in 2016/2017, although we have heard little about them in the intervening period.

More importantly, it is crucial to remember that the Home Secretary shapes the overall nature of HMIFRCS' activities and the framework that forms the basis of its inspection judgements. The continuing lack of national leadership or a realistic long-term vision from the government and the Home Office are perhaps the most disappointing aspects. These shortcomings feed directly into the continuing absence of professional and performance standards and the lack of progress on developing the data, intelligence and information that are needed to deliver and evaluate the service and the safety of the public. These fundamental flaws could and should have been addressed with much greater urgency. One might have expected the disastrous Grenfell Tower fire to provide the necessary catalyst for action. And yet this does not appear to have been the case. What will it take, to have in place arrangements that the public can have confidence in, particularly at a time when Brexit continues to consume national political energy?

Underpinning this neglect is the continuing under-resourcing of the service, which has been a problem common to many public services since the policy of 'austerity localism' was adopted in 2010. Despite pre-election promises of more resources for public services, education, the NHS and the police have commanded the greatest attention, with no mention of fire services in either popular or political discourse. The government's first response to implementing Dame Judith Hackitt's recommendations for strengthening fire safety in construction (MHCLG, 2019) has been to water down her recommendations and transfer some of the regulatory responsibilities of government onto building owners (Harper, 2019; LABC, 2019).

6.5 WHAT SHOULD BE THE REACTION TO THE FINDINGS OF OUR STUDY?

How should we prioritise what the sector needs to do to improve the performance regime? With so much that potentially could be improved and limited resources with which to work, we need to be realistic. We should also be aware that some things can be done quickly, whilst others will take some considerable time.

Firstly, at the national level, it would be extremely helpful if the key stakeholders and particularly the government would make it clear that 'risk' rather than any other factor (such as demand, price or need) is the basis upon which we should configure and evaluate fire and rescue services. In the United Kingdom, fire and rescue is a public service that creates public value in a contested democratic environment (Bennington & Hartley, 2019).

Secondly, fire and rescue services operate within an inherently contested political environment; trust, reciprocity and collaboration are vital to the primary purpose of ensuring public safety. Key stakeholders and partners in such an environment need to have productive long-term relationships and co-create or co-produce policy as well as collaborating in its implementation. This needs to be evidence-based and quality assured if it is to command the confidence of partners and key stakeholders.

Thirdly, our study has highlighted the continuing inadequacy of the evidence base at both national and local levels. It is not an exaggeration to describe progress towards its improvement as dissapointing. The local priority should be IRMPs. We have suggested that this might be a suitable subject for a themed inspection or, perhaps alternatively, a national study, or some combination of both. It could be undertaken with the help of the inspectorate after the first round of service inspections are complete, and the 'state of fire' is reported to the government, but before a new inspection framework timetable and methodology are agreed.

And yet, there are still some positive signs. We retain some hope that key actors will address these three concerns. For example, Suzanne McCarthy, the recently appointed Chair of the Fire Standards Board has said that she intends to work with a range of organisations to create and maintain a suite of standards, which includes the Home Office, the Local Government Association, the Association of Crime and Police Commissioners, and the National Fire Chiefs Council. However, she also said that 'every standard will be evidence-based, will be consulted on and reviewed. It's going to be impact assessed and then when it is put into place it is going to be kept under review' (McCarthy, 2019). This implies changes will not be immediate; indeed, she admitted the board is still in the process of scoping the suite of standards.

Beyond this, the government has announced that it will be including the lessons learnt and outcomes of the Hackitt review within the national framework, as soon as is practical. This will also provide an opportunity to amend and improve the framework, clarify the purpose and role of the government in the sector and update statistics. If this opportunity has not presented itself by late 2019, HMICFRS is due to deliver its 'State of Fire and Rescue' report to the government after the completion of their first round of service inspections, due around the same time. This report may also contribute towards the necessary improvements to the framework. Failing that, the Fire and Rescue Services Act 2004 requires the Secretary of State to report every two years on fire and rescue authorities' compliance with the Fire and Rescue National Framework, with the next report due before July 2020.

Therefore, despite the constraints on public services caused by the twin forces of austerity and Brexit, there should be sufficient opportunities to make further improvements in the national frameworks. Whether this occurs remains to be seen, but we hope that our thoughts and recommendations set out in this book are able to influence the future direction of fire and rescue services. Fire and rescue services often find themselves out of the public spotlight, other than for reasons of disasters or strikes. We contend that is perhaps time that the government, at least, begins to address the challenges the sector faces in a more coherent fashion.

REFERENCES

Benington, J., & Hartley, J. (2019). Public value as a contested democratic practice. In A. Lindgreen, N. Koenig-Lewis, M. Kitchener, J. Brewer, M. Moore & T. Meynhardt (Eds.),

Public value: deepening, enriching and broadening the theory and practice (pp. 143–158). Abingdon: Routledge.

Department of Communities and Local Government. (2008). *Fire and rescue service national framework 2008–11.* Wetherby: Department of Communities and Local Government.

Department of Communities and Local Government (2012). *Fire and rescue national framework for England.* London: Department of Communities and Local Government/TSO.

Ewen, S. (2010). *Fighting fires: Creating the British fire service 1800–1978.* Basingstoke: Palgrave Macmillan.

Ferry, L., & Murphy, P. (2015). *Financial sustainability, accountability and transparency across local public service bodies in England under austerity.* Report to National Audit Office (NAO). Retrieved from http://llr.ntu.ac.uk/rpd/researchpublications.php?pubid=20a41547-5658-4781-9b0c-4a6d3ff9f25a. Accessed on October 31, 2019.

Harper, M. (2019). Grenfell call for action: Facing a safer future. *FIRE, 115*(1420), 40–41.

HM Inspectorate of Constabulary and Fire & Rescue Services. (2018). *Fire and rescue services inspection programme and framework 2018/19.* London: HM Inspectorate of Constabulary and Fire & Rescue Services.

Home Office. (2018). *Fire and rescue national framework for England.* London: Home Office.

Local Authority Building Control. (2019). *Building control matters: Responding to MHCLG's consultation on the Hackitt review implementation. A special briefing edition for local government.* London: Local Authority Building Control.

May, T. (2016). *Home Secretary speech on fire reform.* London: Home Office.

McCarthy, S. (2019). *Speech to Institute of Fire Engineers* International conference 'Professionalism and Ethics in the Fire Sector' Brighton, 17th July 2019. As quoted in FIRE, *115*(1420), p. 46.

Ministry of Housing, Communities and Local Government (2019). *Building a safer future: Proposals for reform of the building safety regulatory system. A consultation.* London: Ministry of Housing, Communities and Local Government.

Murphy, P. (2015a). *Briefing note on 'Financial sustainability of fire and rescue services – local government report' for the National Audit Office.* London: National Audit Office. Retrieved from http://llr.ntu.ac.uk/rpd/researchpublications. php?pubid=20a41547-5658-4781-9b0c-4a6d3ff9f25a

Murphy, P. (2015b). *Briefing note on 'Financial sustainability of fire and rescue services – value for money report' for the National Audit Office.* London: National Audit Office. Retrieved from http://llr.ntu.ac.uk/rpd/researchpublications. php?pubid=20a41547-5658-4781-9b0c-4a6d3ff9f25a

Murphy, P. (2017). Independent inspectorate in danger of becoming Home Office handmaiden. *FIRE, 112*(1398), 9–11.

Murphy, P., Ferry, L., Glennon, R., & Greenhalgh, K. (2019a). *Public service accountability: Rekindling a debate.* Cham: Palgrave Macmillan.

Murphy, P., Lakoma, K., & Toothill, A. (2019b). Do we need to review IRMPs? *FIRE, 114*(1419), 13–16.

National Audit Office. (2015). *Financial sustainability of fire and rescue services, HC 491.* London: National Audit Office.

National Fire Chiefs Council. (2017). *NFCC strategy 2017–2020: Strategic commitment 5.1 assessing community risk*. Birmingham: National Fire Chiefs Council.

Office of the Deputy Prime Minister. (2004). *The fire and rescue service national framework 2004/05*. London: TSO.

Office of the Deputy Prime Minister. (2006). *The fire and rescue service national framework 2006/07*. London: The Stationery Office.

Public Accounts Committee. (2016). *Financial sustainability of fire and rescue services: Twenty-third report of session 2015–16*. London: TSO.

The Police Foundation. (2019). *Strategic review of policing in England and Wales*. Retrieved from http://www.police-foundation.org.uk/project/strategic-review-of-policing/. Accessed on December 16, 2019.

INDEX

Printed in the United States
By Bookmasters